AF206981

Shearing Sheep and Angora Goats the Texas Way

Number Twenty
Clayton Wheat Williams Texas Life Series

Sheep and goat ranching is our family heritage. Every member of my generation and those before me remembers rounding up, working pens, packing wool and mohair as shearers loaded sacks, and eating with crews at their campsites. As I write this tribute, I remember the Robert Cauthorn, Henry Mills, and Pat and Abb Rose families of Val Verde County. Our families, and The Bank & Trust, were built on the sheep and goat industry.

— Sid Cauthorn, CEO
The Bank & Trust and Anco Insurance Managers, Inc.

Shearing Sheep and Angora Goats the Texas Way

Legacy of Pride

Robert Aguero

Foreword by Arnoldo De León

TEXAS A&M UNIVERSITY PRESS
COLLEGE STATION

♾ This paper meets the requirements of ANSI/NISO Z39.48-1992
(Permanence of Paper).
Binding materials have been chosen for durability.

Library of Congress Cataloging-in-Publication Data

Names: Aguero, Robert, 1950– author. |
De León, Arnoldo, 1945– writer of foreword.
Title: Shearing sheep and Angora goats the Texas way : legacy of pride /
Robert Aguero ; foreword by Arnoldo De León.
Other titles: Clayton Wheat Williams Texas life series ; no. 20.
Description: First edition. | College Station : Texas A&M University Press,
[2024] | Series: Clayton Wheat Wlliams Texas life series ; number twenty
| Includes bibliographical references and index.
Identifiers: LCCN 2023024269 | ISBN 9781648431609 (hardcover) |
ISBN 9781648431616 (ebook)
Subjects: LCSH: Aguero, Robert, 1950- | Sheep-shearing—Texas—
History.| Angora goat—Handling—Texas—History. | Sheep-shearing—
Technique. | Sheep shearers (Persons)—Mexico—Equipment and supplies.
| Mexican American agricultural laborers—Texas—History. | BISAC:
SOCIAL SCIENCE / Ethnic Studies / American / Hispanic American
Studies | BIOGRAPHY & AUTOBIOGRAPHY / Cultural, Ethnic &
Regional / Hispanic & Latino
Classification: LCC HD8039.S472 A38 2024 | DDC
636.3/14509764—dc23/eng/20230808
LC record available at https://lccn.loc.gov/2023024269

For John Allen Davis

John Allen Davis Sr. and his prized Angora billy goat. Photograph courtesy of Jad Davis.

The shearers performed their work for more than their livelihood; rather, it was their identity, distinguishing them from other Tejanos who lived on ranches and from those with other trades and skills.

—Andrés Tijerina, *Tejano Empire*

Contents

Chapter Five
Las Máquinas: The Crews
61

Chapter Six
The Tools of the Trade
81

Chapter Seven
Dancing with Sheep and Goats:
The Techniques Used for Shearing in Texas
93

Chapter Eight
Los Tasinques: The Shearers
113

Chapter Nine
Los Rancheros: The Ranchers
133

Chapter Ten
Epilogue: We Were Once Shearers
161

Glossary
173

References
183

Index
187

Foreword

IN THIS CAPTIVATING ACCOUNT, Robert Aguero, an accomplished sheep and goat shearer (*tasinque*) and by profession a college president, preserves for us a much-needed chronicle of the fascinating day-to-day work life of those Mexican Americans who engage in the task of sheep and Angora goat shearing. Concerned over the loss of the shearing trade due to the decline of the sheep and Angora goat industry, the author strives to retain a record of the work done by Mexican American *tasinques* so that "the craft of shearing will not be completely forgotten."

Aguero is a participant-observer in this narrative of Mexican-descent men who make a career of sheep and goat shearing. By no means does he purport to be a trained ethnographer studying subjects in the field, however. Rather, his observations, commentary, and conclusions derive from on-the-scene, firsthand experience working as a tasinque from a young age, then through his high school and college years, and now as a retired college administrator. As a member of his family's crew, Aguero traversed sheep lands from the ranges of West Texas to the mountain states in the US Midwest. His background permits him to speak with credibility about what he witnessed. The world embraced is one of Spanish-speaking, Tex-Mex people whose work as tasinques is yet to be fully explored and wholly elaborated on in the academic literature. The subjects live in a cultural space rooted in *lo mexicano*: their home ambience is Mexican, their food is Mexican, as are their customs and traditions, and certainly the decorum by which they interact with family, the citizenry at large, and in this case, with fellow tasinques. Indeed, the character of the tasinque is conspicuously Mexican—actually, Tex-Mex.

The job domain has a Mexican aura, as one would expect in that sheep shearing has a history traceable to Iberia and Mexico. Workers are either Spanish-language dominant or bilingual, and thus Spanish is the medium of communication on the range, applied to all aspects of the trade. In one of the longest chapters in the book, Aguero acquaints us with the vocabulary of the shearing operation. There is the name identifying the crew (*la companía*), the indispensable tools (*mango, navajas,* and *chinos*), and the shearing machine (*la máquina*). Precise terms specify one's standing in the hierarchical structure (*capitán, pora*). The respective work duty entrusted to each member of the group has fitting designations (*el amolador, el cocinero*). Chores having apt descriptions at the shearing pen are the *lanero, empacador, tecolero,* and *corralero.* Special titles and honor recognition are bestowed on those with exceptional ability (*la espada, tesonero*).

Sheep and Angora goat shearing calls for careful planning and preparation for a long season, order out on the open camp, and resolve to execute brutal work as efficiently as possible. Aguero carefully leads us through every phase of the business, starting with the capitán's efforts to assemble a crew at the point of origin (perhaps Camp Wood, Rocksprings, Sonora, Uvalde, or other areas around the Edwards Plateau region), taking us then along the route of transit on old trucks moving over rough country roads, next to the arrival at the ranch site in South Dakota or Montana, and ultimately to the establishment of a campsite where the shearers improvise at outdoor living. During the course of the travel cycle, the crew develops a certain cohesiveness, somewhat akin to that historians associate with sports teams, vaquero units, oil field hands, and smelter workers. An esprit de corps shapes work rhythms, sharpens craftsmanship, and reinforces one's work ethic. Cultural background establishes the informal roles for the playful interaction in which the tasinques engage, including kidding, nicknaming, lampooning, and what the participants know as *jugando pesado*. But never far from the tasinques' goals is seeing to their families' material improvement and to ensuring the social advancement of their children, for despite the nature of the job, most are bicultural and true believers in the nation's creed.

This book, focusing on one more aspect of the multifaceted life of Texas Mexicans, strengthens the body of scholarship that continues to pour out in Mexican American studies. It is a fitting addition to established fields such as social history, describing a community of ordinary people going about life with dignity as Hispanic Americans. It is a labor history, shedding light on still another mass of workers such as cotton pickers and migrants in the beet fields, contending with arduous toil. It is archival history; its inclusion of oral interviews of former *tasinques* parallels programs such as the "Voces Oral History Project" at the University of Texas and the collection of remembrances in Marcia Hatfield Daudistel and Mimi R. Gladstein's *The Women of Smeltertown*. Last, it can be considered a contribution to the history of photography. The author has carefully selected pictures to counter the usual representation of sheep shearers "as sweating men bent over with arched backs and heads down," and like other Mexican workers, anonymous to history. The optics come from the Robert Aguero Photo Collection and Russell Lee Photograph Collection at the Dolph Briscoe Center for American History.

Others have written about Mexican American sheep shearers, but none with the personal perspective, the insight, and *corazón* of our author.

—Arnoldo De León

Acknowledgments

I would like to express my sincere appreciation to all of the interviewees who gave me their time and energy so I could record the shearing industry as they remembered it.

My sincere thanks also go to the Uvalde Public Library for allowing me access to its wonderful treasure trove of documents and photographs of the shearing industry.

I also wish to thank all the shearers and crew captains with whom I worked for more than ten years. They all provided me with work, great knowledge, guidance, and wonderful memories throughout my time in the sheep and Angora goat–shearing industry, *la trasquila*.

Last, thanks to my wife, Olivia, for putting up with my long hours of work on this project and for her endless encouragement.

Introduction

IN READING MARGIE CRISP'S BOOK *The Nueces River*, I identified keenly with the geographical setting, the Nueces River Valley of Texas. The book struck home since I grew up swimming in the Nueces River, which winds itself around my hometown of Camp Wood. Most important, Crisp's method of conveying stories about ranchers and rural life around the river was inspiring. I also identified keenly with the people and their work in Ken Roberts's book *The Cedar Choppers*, which describes the cedar-chopping industry that still exists in the Nueces River Valley and describes vividly the working lives of the cedar choppers themselves.

Collectively, both books inspired me to write of another unique industry and rural life that I experienced and participated in during my early years growing up in the Nueces River Valley. It was an industry that at one time was hugely important to Texas and the ranchers and shearers who made a living from it. That industry was sheep and Angora goat shearing, or *la trasquila*, as we knew it. I felt that the industry's story needed to be told since, sadly, the shearing industry has almost disappeared.

Stories of an industry and its people can perhaps best be told in pictures; thus, I have included many in this book that represent great examples of the heart of the industry, the actual shearing of the animal, the men involved, and the tools utilized. Famed photographer Russell Lee took photographs for a study that George Sanchez conducted for the University of Texas at Austin in 1949. This one depicts a typical shearing crew of that time period. Typical of many photographs taken of sheep and goat shearing, it depicts well the work but does not identify or say much about the shearers and their coworkers because they are usually bent over with arched backs and heads down. So a major part of this

Sheep shearers on a ranch near Sonora, Texas, 1949. Russell Lee Photograph Collection, e_rl_14233r1_0007, The Dolph Briscoe Center for American History, The University of Texas at Austin.

book is focused on identifying the shearers as well as the other people involved in the shearing crews.

I have purposely provided as many of the names of individuals involved in the shearing crews and the industry as possible. It was done so that the names of Mexican American tasinques and the craft of shearing will not be completely forgotten as the shearing industry recedes into history.

Another outstanding feature of the 1949 Sanchez study is that it vividly and brilliantly conveyed the shearing industry through pictures. It can be seen that the photograph captured in still form the intricate choreography involved in handling the animal and positioning to remove its mohair or wool as quickly and safely as possible—safely for the animal and the shearer. The photo also captured the smooth strokes necessary to shear the animal cleanly and the tools necessary to do the work. Those features were also part of the culture of the shearing industry. The culture included extensive travel, large and small crews, unique foods, a language of its own, the necessary tools, a very specific technique, and literally the lives of the men who did the work. Therefore, one part of the book is dedicated to describing this culture.

A unique aspect of this book is that it is being written by a shearer, the person being photographed, not the photographer. Therefore, the book is written from the perspective of a person who actually did the work of shearing sheep and Angora goats, spoke its unique language, ate its unique foods, lived its culture, and for a brief time made a living doing the difficult work. Further, it is an inside look at the work itself as done in the Texas style: its tools, its techniques, and its compensation. In essence, it seeks to provide an insight into the very difficult task of making a living in the shearing industry.

As I began work on this book, I found myself adopting a sort of technical- and research-oriented approach. But I soon realized that to tell the story well, I needed to write *con corazón* (with heart). For you see, the climate and ambience of the work was done with heart. In order to write con corazón, I use stories about the industry and much of the language of the industry.

The book is divided into two major sections. The first two chapters give a brief history of the shearing industry as it was written by others: in essence, using secondary sources. The last chapters are dedicated to my experiences as a sheep and Angora goat shearer. My stories are the memories and notes I have kept over the years. I use the words *trasquila* and *tasinque* to refer to the industry and the shearers, respectively. The formal words are *trasquiladura* and *trasquilador*. I used the more informal words simply because that is how we knew them and how they were used in the industry and in Texas for over a hundred years. Additionally, I refer to shearers as Mexicans only if they were or are from Mexico. I refer to shearers as Hispanic or Mexican Americans if they were apparently native-born Americans.

Finally, it is my hope that I convey well the "art" of shearing sheep and Angora goats. The graceful, smooth hand movements; the choreography of the feet; the fusion of balance with the animal; the ripple of strength of the shearer; and the exertion evidenced during the dance-like performance are all part of the "aesthetic subtleties" that I hope to capture.

Shearing Sheep and Angora Goats the Texas Way

1

A Brief History of Shearing and the Shearers

THERE ARE MANY OCCUPATIONS that are purported to be the oldest professions known to humanity, and sheep and goat shearing can stake a claim to being one of the oldest. References to shearers can be found as early as biblical times. For instance, Genesis 38:12–13 says, "Judah went up to his shearers at Timnah. It was told to Tamar, 'Behold, your father-in-law is going to Timnah to shear his sheep.'" Additionally, Samuel 22:23 speaks of Nabal and his shearers: "Now it came about after two full years that Absalom had sheep shearers in Ball-hazar. When David heard that in the desert Nabal was shearing his flock, he said, I have heard that your shearers are with you. . . . Nabal said to David, must I take my bread, my wine, my meat that I have slaughtered for my own shearers, and give it to men who come from I know not where?"

Indeed, these verses cite the fact that shearing has existed from time immemorial as a profession that continues to this day. The sheep and goats have survived and persisted over the centuries, providing consistent sources of food and clothing for humanity. Sheep and goat shearing in the Americas is not quite as old as in the land of Judah and David, but it is at least five hundred years old. Its history dates back to Christopher Columbus's arrival in the New World. A year after his epic voyage of 1492, he returned to the New World, known in Europe as the Americas, and this time brought sheep and goats (Carlson 1982).

Early introduction of sheep into present-day Texas began with an incursion by Francisco Vázquez de Coronado. In 1540 he led a large number of men, horses, cattle, hogs, and sheep into western Texas, looking for the mythical "Seven Cities of Cibola" that were rumored to have streets paved with gold. Although Coronado ventured into the palisaded plains (Llano Estacado) of Texas, he did not find the Seven Cities, much less any gold. He returned to Mexico with a failed expedition but did leave much of his stock in Texas. Some of it multiplied greatly (Duran and Bernard 1973).

By 1667 in Nuevo León, a northern territory of New Spain, stockmen founded *haciendas* with thousands of sheep, and by 1736 there were some 1.5 million sheep there. Spaniards established the province of Tejas in 1718, which extended north to Louisiana and south to the Nueces River. Land south of the Nueces River was in the province of Nuevo Santander, in the middle of which was the Rio Grande. Thus, the coastal plains of Texas, vast lands in the Southwest, the prairies of West Texas, and large portions of northern Mexico provided immense grazing lands for sheep. By 1757 stockmen and their vast haciendas in these areas continued to add great numbers of sheep (Arreola 2002).

As haciendas and sheep ranching developed, great empires grew from the sheep industry and the availability of vast expanses of grazing lands.

Sheep grazing at Iron Mountain Ranch in Buchel County, Texas. From Salmon (1892, 946).

For example, the Sanchez-Navarro empire, known as a *latifundio*, was established in 1765 and lasted more than a hundred years. It was located in the state of León, which consisted of present-day northern Mexico and parts of Texas. The empire at one time consisted of many haciendas over some 2.2 million acres, all under one ownership, much like the famous later Texas empire of the King Ranch. The latifundio had to have its 250,000 sheep sheared and during this time employed shearers from the settlements of Monclova in the state of Tlascala, Mexico (Harris 1975).

By the 1860s there existed many crews of sheep shearers (*tasinques*), who typically dressed in overalls with a bandanna on their head and arrived on a horse (*caballo*). Each crew was fifty or sixty strong with a captain (*capitán*) who was the crew boss. The crews made the great circle of shearing pens from Texas to California and throughout the Rocky Mountain states. The shearers would "live and work on the ranch for more than a month, so many were the sheep to be sheared" (McWilliams 1990, 141).

By 1865 the Civil War had ended and

> dreamers, entrepreneurs, US immigrants, and farmers moved themselves and their families into Texas and the lands along the Nueces River and its tributaries. The settlers brought sheep. Hundreds of thousands of sheep flooded the plains of the Rio Grande. Between 1860 and the early 1880s, the population of sheep exploded. An estimated 1.7 million sheep grazed in the mesquite prairies, and nearly half of all sheep in Texas were south of the Nueces River (Crisp 2017, 128).

In the 1870s and 1880s ranchers expanded the sheep industry into West Texas. Charles Schreiner of Kerrville was credited as the greatest source for expanding the sheep industry in Texas during this time and into the 1890s. His system of commissions for wool sales expanded the sale of wool throughout the United States. Thus, by 1900 every county in Texas had sheep, but the greatest concentration was in the Edwards Plateau, and by 1943 Texas had 10.8 million sheep (Carlson 2010).

And of course, the shearers followed the sheep. V. W. Lehman quotes Walter W. Meek from a letter Meek wrote from Las Hermanitas Ranch near present-day Freer to his fiancée in 1887. In his letter, Meek presented a brief description of shearing and shearers: "Mexicans do the shearing

Sheep grazing by the Devil's River in West Texas. From Salmon (1892, 946).

of course—say about twenty men do the cutting. . . . One man will cut the wool off about forty sheep in a day." Thus, they worked up to fifteen days to shear all of the ranch's sheep. They were paid two cents per head including board (Lehman 1969, 59). Meek also indicated that the men would tie down five sheep at a time on the floor of the pen.

The exponential growth of sheep ranching resulted in more crews of organized sheep shearers. The crews worked their way north through the Mexican states of Jalisco, Durango, Chihuahua, and Sonora. The early crews were Indians or Mexicans and were led by the captain who initiated the contracts, billed the rancher for the shearing, and enforced discipline (Wentworth 1948).

As the shearing became more of a business and more readily available, ranchers such as Helen Hunt Jackson started to notice the shearing techniques and began recording them in writing:

> The thirty shearers, running into the nearest pen, dragged each sheep into the shed. In the twinkling of an eye he had the creature between his knees, helpless, immovable, and the sharp sound of the shears set in. . . . As soon as a sheep was shorn, the shearer ran with the fleece in his hand to Luigo, threw it down on a table, received his five-cent piece, dropped it in his pocket, ran to the pen, dragged out another sheep, and in less than five minutes was back with a second fleece (Quoted in Wentworth 1948, 420).

The photograph depicts the "shears" that the shearers used to remove the fleeces. The packer is on top of the wood contraption used to pack the wool in sacks; however, he had to stomp it down with his feet to firmly pack it into the sacks. Some of the more fortunate shearers, probably due to seniority, can be seen shearing under the shed, which provided cover from the hot sun. Vivid descriptions were also written of such scenes:

> The shearing was done in a large pen covered with brush, reeds, or pal-metto . . . and roofed with shingles, capable of giving shelter . . . and then have room for thirty men to work. At daybreak all hands assembled in the pen. Every man had a number of rawhide strings to tie the feet of the sheep as he laid them down ready for shearing. Each man as a rule tied ten sheep at a time. A man with a book and pencil kept tally of the number of sheep tied down by the shearers. Another man stood at a table with a ball of twine, received and tied up each fleece separately. By the side of the table a sack attached to a round ring to keep it open, and placed in a frame, received each fleece as it was tied. Each sack when well packed held about 360 pounds, and when filled was weighed and was ready for the market. (Lehmann 1969, 63).

The practice of dragging sheep, and later Angora goats, by their hind leg persists to this day, and it was an intricate skill that had to be learned

Mexican sheep shearers near Fort McKavett, Texas. From Salmon (1892, 946).

if the shearer was to position the animal well at the shearing station without harming it.

By 1884 it was not uncommon to see hundreds of shearers on each ranch. They came from Mexico twice a year, from April until the end of September, as teams with each group having its own captain who maintained order and discipline and made the contracts with the ranchers and shearers. The contracts generally specified terms of wages and accommodations. The shearers crossed the border in large numbers, as indicated in an account quoted by Arnoldo De León: "The *tasinques* (shearers) headed for the South Texas counties or as far as Llano County. This makes over 400 shearers that have passed through Eagle Pass in the last week, reported an Eagle Pass correspondent in April 1884" (1982, 60).

By 1885 some of the crews originated from Texas. A newspaper article written in that year indicated that the shearers came from Uvalde and other border towns. Some of the men arrived on burros and ponies, but the larger number arrived on a "prairie schooner." The men were described as dark and black-eyed, and they traveled in "jolly spirits." Though they may have been a happy bunch, according to the article the men were also armed with Winchesters, and some may have had engaged in "homicides." The article goes to great pains to describe the men as "ready to kill" if needed, only hanging up their weapons when ready to start work (Murphy 2019).

Special Report on the History and Present Condition of the Sheep Industry in the United States, 1892, commissioned by the US Department of Agriculture, cited how much the sheep industry had spread throughout the United States by 1892. It found that almost every US state had some sheep farming or ranching. Most states had few sheep, and the owners themselves generally did the shearing. However, Montana had 2,827,714 sheep, and Utah reported 2,800,000 sheep. Additionally, Texas had twenty-two counties listed, including Sutton, Edwards, Menard, Tom Green, and Concho, which combined had more than 1,100,000 sheep (Salmon 1892).

Although it was not conducted for the purpose of reporting on shearing per se, the special report did indicate that shearing was alive and well in the United States. For instance, in Southwest Texas counties, shearing was done twice a year, generally in the spring and summer. In 1892, the shearing was still done mostly by men from Mexico in crews that consisted of ten to forty shearers. Their pay was now up to five cents per head, and board was provided. The special report also described notable scenes at the shearing pens: "On the arrival of a band of shearers, a few loose boards are placed on the ground, and the sheep are caught and quickly divested of their fleeces, which are tied up separately and placed in sacks of 200 pounds each." The study specifically noted that the sheep by this time were mostly the Merino breed (Salmon 1892, 138).

The early 1900s saw shearing crews flourish in Texas, and it was obvious that the shearers were now in large part Mexican Americans, not only men from Mexico. For instance, in the 1930s several captains made

Merino ram "Don Pedro." From Salmon (1892, 134).

their homes in San Angelo. The captains sheared in Texas but did venture with their crews to northern states such as Colorado and Montana. Their negotiated contracts with ranchers, generally oral agreements, contained provisions for pricing, for the rancher to provide meat for the shearers, and for agreement on the date the shearing was to occur. Agreements also had to be reached between the captain and the shearer, who often required advanced pay (*reganche*). The captain agreed to provide the shearing rig, but the shearer provided his own tools.

The crews consisted of as many as twenty shearers. Each could average about one hundred sheep per day at an average of three cents per head: approximately thirty dollars per week. "In those days that was big money," one shearer indicated at the time (Guerrero 1991, 43). The money in advance was indeed an integral part of the shearing industry. Also, the tradition of the rancher providing the meat (*carne*) was always important and persisted through the 1990s.

A less formal description of the shearing culture in Texas comes from the 1930s. Although brief, it provides a vignette of how the tradition of shearing was sometimes passed on from generation to generation. However, the brief description provides evidence of another cultural phenomenon quite prevalent in the Hispanic communities in Texas, and including the shearing industry. It was an honorable, yet costly tradition of young men dropping out of school to help their families subsist. While attending Sul Ross State University in Alpine, Bertha Dominguez of Del Rio wrote of her grandfather, Welito, and her father:

> Welito had to work to help out for a while . . . and at the age of twenty-two, he decided to go out on his own and become a sheep shearer. . . . Welito worked hard to get ahead, and soon had his own shearing machine (this was in the 1930s). When my dad, Sixto Rodriquez, Jr. was sixteen years old . . . it was time for him to quit school and start earning a living by helping Welito out . . . and Dad left school his junior year, to work with Welito full time in the shearing camps (Dominquez 2004, 62).

By 1945 shearing mechanization was undergoing drastic changes. New machines replaced "hand shears," which were described as "contrivances resembling a barber's clippers." As many as twenty shearers would line up "along a line shaft." This meant the shearers no longer bunched up in the pen and tied as many as ten animals at a time; rather, they now kept a pen full (*atajo*) of sheep in front of them and selected one animal at a time. The headpieces were now attached to "drops" (the shearers' stations) that were "like a robot dangling long, loose jointed arms" that reached to the shearing floor, and a clipper was attached to each arm, which was in turn attached to pulleys and belts that generated the power for the tools (Kupper 1945, 158). The hand shears were now replaced by the new "headpieces" that now included a comb (*chino*) and cutters (*navajas*) that did the actual cutting of the fleece.

The new mechanization era now necessitated more shearers who had to learn a completely new set of shearing skills. For example, maneuvering the new headpiece allowed the shearer to work much faster than when using the hand shears, but the headpiece brought added costs for the shearers and introduced a new element of danger of cutting the animal or the shearer himself.

Shearing in the 1940s continued in a very regular fashion, and the shearing industry in the San Angelo area was typical of the times. Because so many men joined the war effort during World War II, Texas shearers were hard to find.

Three headpieces (*mangos*) resembling a barber's clippers and two "scissor shears." Photograph courtesy of the Crockett County Historical Museum, Ozona, Texas.

Sheep shearers on a ranch near Sonora, Texas, 1949, each lined up "along the line shaft" and working from a steel drop. Russell Lee Photograph Collection, e_rl_14233r1_0007, The Dolph Briscoe Center for American History, The University of Texas at Austin.

Calls went out yearly from local ranchers for *tasinques*. The greatest demand occurred from March through May, when goats were being sheared and the kidding season and the wool clipping were underway, while there was less urgent demand around September when some sheep were clipped a second time. During World War I . . . shearers from Mexico were made available for West Texas ranchers. Locally, men who supplied part of this labor were *enganchistas* (De León 1985, 34).

Ranchers continued regular use of *enganchistas*, a term derived from *enganche* (more frequently called *reganche*), which involved advancing payment to the shearers before the shearing season, but at times ranchers also provided it to the captain. In both instances the contracts were generally sealed with a handshake and nothing else.

A most informative study, *The Study of the Spanish-Speaking People of Texas*, commissioned by University of Texas professor George I. Sanchez and directed by sociologist Lyle Saunders, was conducted in Texas in 1948–49. The goal was to investigate social aspects of prejudice and discrimination against the Spanish-speaking people of the state. Russell

Lee, acclaimed professional photographer, took some nine hundred photographs that capture in an excellent fashion the "many poignant, proud, exasperating, joyful, and intimate moments in the lives of people in these Mexican American communities at a very specific point in time" (Sanchez 1949).

Although the study was not specifically about shearing or the shearing industry in Texas, Russell Lee photographically documented the profession in Texas as it was carried out by Mexican Americans. Lee took some extraordinary photographs of men shearing sheep near the town of Sonora, about sixty-five miles south of San Angelo, in 1949. The photographs depict the tools, the sheep, the atmosphere, and the men involved in the industry at that time. Unfortunately, the men are not identified. The images show that the work required the shearers to be bent over with their heads down all day as they sheared each animal. A large tarp draped over the truck and men provided shade, but it was very hot, dirty work in the summer months. Historically, just as Mexican men did the work in the early years, mostly only Mexican American (Hispanic) men did the shearing at the time of the study.

Sheep shearers on a ranch near Sonora, 1949. The individual belts run from the pulleys of the steel shaft to the individual drops. Russell Lee Photograph Collection, e_rl_14233r2_0016, The Dolph Briscoe Center for American History, The University of Texas at Austin.

These photographs portray vividly how shearing was done from the
1940s until about the mid-1960s. The men are lined up along the shearing
machine (*la máquina*) that generated the power needed to drive their
tools. Generally, another row of men would be located on the other side
of the truck, so the crew probably totaled ten or twelve men. A pen full

Sheep shearers on a ranch near Sonora, 1949. Russell Lee Photograph Collection,
e_rl_14233_0018, The Dolph Briscoe Center for American History, The University of
Texas at Austin.

Sheep shearer securing the comb and cutters to the headpiece on a ranch near Sonora, 1949. Russell Lee Photograph Collection, e_rl_14233r2_0028, The Dolph Briscoe Center for American History, The University of Texas at Austin.

Sheep shearer tying a sheep to shear it safely on a ranch near Sonora, 1949. Russell Lee Photograph Collection, e_rl_14233r2_0017, The Dolph Briscoe Center for American History, The University of Texas at Austin.

Frijolillos depicting the number of tokens collected by a shearer. Photograph from author's collection.

of sheep was kept in front of them from which shearers could select and drag each animal to their individual stations to be sheared.

The engine that powered the tools, the *ingenio*, was built onto a flatbed truck that could be driven from ranch to ranch as the shearing season progressed. The motor itself, which cannot be clearly seen in the photos, sat on the floor of the truck. On some machines, the truck's own engine powered the pulleys. From a pulley attached to the engine, a belt ran up to the steel shaft, from which other pulleys ran belts that were attached to each shearing drop. The belts turned a clutch that in turn rotated a set of small gears in the clutch, providing the power to each drop and thus each headpiece. The overall machine was in later years placed on a trailer, thus eliminating the need for the truck. At the cutting edge of each headpiece were a comb and cutter that actually did the cutting. The comb and cutters had to be kept razor-sharp at all times by the man who sharpened the cutters, known as *el amolador.*

In other countries such as Australia and New Zealand, the sheep are sheared without being tied. This technique made its way farther into the United States each season; however, the technique of tying the sheep and goats is still the most prevalent method for shearing in Texas. This method originated when shearers tied as many as ten sheep at a time

Captain counting sheep as they leave the pen on a ranch near Sonora, 1949. Russell Lee Photograph Collection, (*l*) e_rl_ 14233r2_0029 and (*r*) e_rl_14233r2_0030, The Dolph Briscoe Center for American History, The University of Texas at Austin.

when they were still shearing with hand shears. The skill and method were passed on to later generations in Texas.

Another important part of the shearing day was counting the animals that had been sheared. For every sheep that was sheared, the shearer was handed a token such as a washer, coin, specialized tin token, or even a red mountain laurel bean (*frijolillo*). The tokens were arranged in rows of ten so the captain could easily see the number of animals sheared by the shearer. The shearer kept count of all of the sheep he sheared in one day in this manner.

Another method of keeping count of the animals sheared during the day was for the captain to count them as they left the shearing pen. He quickly counted by twos and got closer to the sheep as they ran out of the pen. This made them less likely to bunch up, which made them more difficult to count accurately.

The sheep were counted after each pen full was sheared so that the number reached by this method could be reconciled with the number of tokens the men received during the day. The rancher also counted the total number of sheep sheared during the day to reconcile with the count that the captain had reached. If all three counts did not reconcile, the rancher and the captain had to come to some agreement. If the captain's count did not reconcile with the total number of tokens submitted by the shearers each day, then the captain had a problem. It was either his miscount, or the men were not being honest.

Meanwhile, as the sheared sheep were leaving the pen and being counted, the shearers might take a break to drink some water, grab a smoke, and chat about the work before the next group of sheep was herded into the pen. This went on all day, every week, every month, and every shearing season, and for some men, all of their working lives. As the sheared sheep were going out of the pen, another pen full of sheep to be sheared would be brought in, and the shearing would start all over again.

The shearing technique in the 1960s and 1970s remained the same, and the pay increased gradually and slowly. In 1964 shearers typically earned between fifteen and twenty cents per head of sheep sheared. However, mechanization again changed in the 1970s, as the belt-driven pulleys were replaced by electric motors that powered the headpieces.

During this time gas- or diesel-powered generators replaced the engine that had been on the shearing ingenio and later on the trailer. The generator was now placed outside the barn or shearing pens. This change meant that at last the smoke, heat, and intense noise from the engine were now outside the shearing pen and away from the shearers. The long drops, headpieces, combs, cutters, and shearing technique still remained basically the same.

By 1992 change was looming for the sheep and Angora goat industry. The legislative elimination of the National Wool Act of 1954 created a precipitous drop-off in US sheep production. Sometimes referred as the Incentive Program, the act required that tariffs be collected on imported raw processed wool, and the tariffs then went into a pool that annually generated ninety million to one hundred million dollars for US wool producers. The US government distributed the tariff funds in the form of a subsidy payment, and this provided a critical safety net for the ranchers. To calculate the share of the pool to pay to producers, the government determined the total number of imported pounds of wool, charged a tariff on them, divided those tariff dollars out less what the government

Chavel Sanchez (*forefront*) and Gilbert Valenzuela utilizing the electric motors on the Davis Ranch near Rio Frio, Texas, 2019. Photograph courtesy of Jad Davis.

kept, and sent the remainder to the wool producers, depending on how much wool they individually produced and the price they received for it (Wilkes 2018).

The Incentive Program was developed to help wool producers, who had to compete with foreign governments that subsidized wool producers in their respective countries. When the program ended, US wool producers did not stand a chance against other subsidized countries, and the demise of an industry began. Unavoidably, the domino effect was devastating, all the way down to the shearers. Additionally, competition with synthetic fibers, drought, predation, an aging ranch population, large land purchases for nonranching use, and labor issues and shortages contributed to the decline (Brezosky 2018a, C1).

Eventually, as the number of sheep and goats in Texas declined, so did the number of shearers. Young Hispanic men became more educated and found more job opportunities in the diverse economy of Texas, including the well-paying oil industry. The shearing tradition was almost completely lost, and it could not be regained overnight, since shearing well enough to make a living and well enough to shear thousands of sheep and goats required many years of laborious development of needed skills.

Recently a newspaper article appeared concerning Severo Soto and Pete Estrada, both in their late seventies, who started shearing in their teenage years. They both still shear at the livestock yards in northwest San Angelo, but they know they will soon retire. Once retirement comes, they believe there will not be any more sheep shearers in San Angelo, once a center for producing shearers. Severo remembers when there were more than twenty crews in San Angelo alone. According to the two men, there are now very few sheep to shear—maybe eighty per day—and no young people to take up the work. In fact, they report that some young people do try shearing, but after a day or so, they leave since the work is just too difficult (Murphy 2019).

Perhaps quite indicative of the shearing industry decline is a story told by a shearing crew captain from Camp Wood. Emerging from a convenience store on an early morning, he encountered a fellow shearing captain from Rocksprings. The friends exchanged greetings. "Are you still shearing these days?" asked the Camp Wood captain. The Rocksprings captain responded, "Yes. But there are not many animals to shear these days and very few shearers left, too." "Which reminds me," the Rocksprings captain continued, "I need to get going, because I need to get all these old shearers back before the nursing home closes." One could hear the friendly cursing directed at the captain from the back of the truck.

Eddie Van Winkle shearing Angora goats on a ranch near Sonora, October 2020. Photograph from author's collection.

2

A Brief History Continued
Shearing the Angora Goat

IN THE EARLY DAYS OF RAISING Angora goats, it was said that if you put three Angora goats each in a barrel, covered the barrels, and a day later uncovered them, three things would have happened: you would find that one goat had died, one had worms, and one had gotten out. The story speaks of the great challenges of raising Angora goats for a living; however, the ranchers were persistent, the goats were resilient, and a giant Texas Angora goat industry was established. It has survived for over 150 years.

Shearing goats and using the hair for cloth also has an ancient story. In biblical times, for instance, as seen in Exodus 4:25, Moses directed that articles of goats' hair be brought to the tabernacle. He directed that the dwelling and its furnishings be made of "gold, silver, . . . fine linen, and goat hair." In Exodus 4:26, Moses further directed, "Also make sheets woven of goats' hair to be used as a tent covering for the dwelling."

Moses's goats were probably not Angora goats, since the Angora goat is thought to have been domesticated by the eighth millennium, perhaps in Asia or Africa. However, it is documented that Angora goats were developed as a breed in what is present-day Turkey and got their name from the region called Ankaras. They were described as "small, refined, delicate animals of great beauty, clipping from two to four pounds of dazzling white, fine, soft, silky, and very lustrous mohair" (Shelton 1993, 5).

Greek authors during the Classic period also mentioned the goat as a domestic animal that produced fine hair. They cited Aelian mentioning the practice of shearing the goats of Lycia in the same manner as sheep

Angora billy kid. Sketch by Mary Ross
Buchholz of Eldorado, Texas, October 2020.
Sketch courtesy of Mary Ross Buchholz.

were sheared and said the wool (hair) was used to make cords and cables. However, not until 1555 was the Angora goat distinctly made known through the writings of Father Belon, a student of ancient Roman times who traveled to Asia Minor and studied Latin and Greek inscriptions. He wrote in his *Observations*, "They breed the finest goats in the world in the region of Angora. They are of a dazzling white, and their hair, which is fine as naturally curled in locks of eight or nine inches long, is worked up into the finest stuffs" (quoted in Hayes 1868, 23). This implies that to get the curled locks "worked up into the finest stuffs," someone had to have sheared the goats. Hayes wrote that indeed a certain Captain Conelly, an English traveler, wrote of his travels in Angora: "The shearing which takes place in April is hardly concluded when the vegetation called forth by the spring is arrested" (25).

Hayes concluded his book by saying that within a half century, the Merino (sheep) was all over the prairies of the West, and in a shorter period the Durham Shorthorn had been acquired and perfected, so "the hope then is not in vain that the precious race [the Angora goat], whose slow march westward we have traced from the remote East, may at no distant time be fully secured for the western world" (1868, 38). His hope was quite prescient, as Angora goats grew to number in the millions in the Western world and especially in the United States.

The formal establishment of Angora goats in the United States occurred during the administration of President James K. Polk (1845–49).

Responding to the request of the sultan of Turkey that an expert come to Turkey to experiment with the production of cotton, President Polk sent James B. Davis of South Carolina. The cotton experiment was so successful that in 1849 the sultan gifted Davis with nine choice goats: seven does (nannies, or female goats) and two bucks (billy goats, or males). Accordingly, the Mohair Council of America (n.d.) records that Davis first brought Angoras to the United States. Consequently, by the time the Civil War began, a number of Angora flocks were scattered through the South and Southwest, and after the war they moved into Texas.

Angora nanny (female) goats on the Davis Ranch near Leakey, Texas, October 2020. Photograph from author's collection.

The first introduction of Angoras to Texas occurred in 1863 in Austin with herds of twelve to three hundred goats. However, the most significant early breeder was William Landrum of Laguna, located between Uvalde and Camp Wood at the intersection of Highways 55 and 334. Landrum purchased goats from Colonel Richard Peters of Atlanta in 1872. At one time, Landrum and a partner had more goats than anyone else in the United States (Stovall 1952).

Imported Angoras also came from South Africa in 1886. G. A. Hoerle of New Jersey made one of the most notable purchases. After petitioning the US Department of Agriculture (USDA), he was allowed to bring into the country 40 or 50 bucks and 120 does with their kids. However, it seems that the last shipment from Turkey or South Africa occurred on May 7, 1925, when 117 Angoras arrived in New York. The animals were then sent to Camp Wood and sold at auction. From that importation and those that occurred between 1863 and 1925, Angora goats grew to a population of four million by 1968 (Stovall 1952).

William Landrum's home in Laguna was located in the Nueces River Valley, later known as the Nueces Canyon. In Texas' early days Spaniards first referred to the canyon as *El Cañon*. Alonso de León then bestowed the name Río de las Nueces, "Pecan River" (Crisp 2017, 128).

Anna Stoner was an early Nueces Canyon pioneer and Angora goat rancher. In 1884 her husband, Clinton, died on their ranch on Hackberry Creek. She sold the ranch and bought 320 acres south of Montell near the now-abandoned town of Good Luck. Widowed and with her two young children, she survived by various means, including shearing her own five hundred Angora goats (Crisp 2017).

Another region of Texas, the Edwards Plateau, became a haven, if not heaven, for Angora goats. The mesquite prairies, fine grasses, and brush country found in the Edwards Plateau were almost perfect for Angora goat ranching. The plateau rises about two thousand feet above the coastal plains and is considered the "Hill Country" of Texas. It has limestone cliffs, rocky pastures, and many woody plants favored by Angora goats as forage. The geologic formation ranges from about seventy-five miles north of San Antonio to about thirty miles south of San Angelo. The Angora headquarters for the plateau may well have been Rocksprings, located in Edwards County. Between 1940 and 1980, 95 percent of the Angoras and mohair production occurred on the plateau (Mohair Council of America, n.d.).

An event that further led to the establishment of the Angora goat in Texas began in 1884. J. W. Jennings of New York City circulated the *Prospectus of the Edwards County Goat and Sheep Ranch*, which outlined a plan for investment in the goat business and proposed that ten persons enter into the organization of a colony in Edwards County. For an investment of five thousand dollars, each investor would receive a lot consisting of 1,280 acres. Each person would also receive two thousand Angora goats. Records are not available about how successful the venture was, but it became evident that many families did create landholdings that led to the Edwards County and Nueces Canyon areas becoming the center of the goat-raising industry (Stovall 1967).

A number of families helped establish the Angora goat in the Nueces Canyon and Edwards Plateau. For instance, Joe Frazier Brown came to Edwards County and helped organize the county in 1883. He was one of the first ranchers to introduce Angora goats there. Goats were selling then for $1.50 to $2.00 per head. By 1903 W. B. Kirchner was an Angora breeder of considerable prominence. He extended his ranch holdings on Spring Creek west of Barksdale and later became associated with the Weaver family in the breeding of fine registered Angora stock. He once made a trip to El Paso and purchased one hundred purebred nannies (Stovall 1967).

The value of mohair grew, selling for fifty-five cents per pound during 1903, as reported by L. S. Friday, foreman of the JWJ Ranch. But by 1919 the average price of mohair had fallen to forty-nine cents per pound. The average price for kid hair, which is always higher, was fifty-eight cents, and the spring clip paid fifty-seven cents. In 1932, however, 850,000 pounds of mohair were sold for anywhere from six to twenty-three cents per pound. Then the price rebounded, and in 1949 mohair sold for forty-two to sixty-two cents per pound. Good times persisted, and in 1951 mohair sold for $1.90 and $2.40 per pound (Stovall 1967).

In the early 1900s about 90 percent of Angora goats were found in Texas, although they were also present in other states such as New Mexico. Their primary range was the Edwards Plateau. Data provided by the Mohair Council of America give an excellent picture of just how Angoras had prospered in the United States, especially in Texas. The numbers ranged from 1,340,000 in 1909, to 2,556,000 in 1926. Edwards County continued to be the leader in the production of Angora goats in Texas. By 1978 it was the number-one county followed, in order, by Val

Verde, Uvalde, and Sutton Counties. Other counties included in the list were Kimble, Terrell, Mason, Crockett, Mills, and Menard in tenth place (Mohair Council of America, n.d.).

Texas benefited greatly as mohair became valuable for its use in fine clothing and other coverings. These products and Angora goat meat had a tremendous impact on the welfare of the entire state. T. R. Fehrenbach cited the importance of Angora goats and sheep to the welfare of Texas:

> Sheep and goat raising also came to Texas in the years following the Civil War, again creating a large enterprise in a similar fashion [as cotton]. Once the Merino sheep and the Angora goat became established in the Hill Country west of San Antonio, the disgust of cattlemen notwithstanding, that city became the wool and mohair capital of the nineteenth-century world (1983, 54).

The development of the "mohair capital" and of mohair production in general was impacted tremendously by two legislative actions. The first occurred during the 1912 session of Congress. Congressman John Nance Garner of Uvalde, although out of step with his party, which

Angora goats on the Davis Ranch near Leakey, October 2020. Photograph from author's collection.

argued for a free market, argued for a tariff protection for goat ranchers. He was a member of the Ways and Means Committee but was voted down on a proposed tariff on imported wool. He succeeded, however, with legislation that imposed a 10 percent ad valorem tariff on imported mohair. Garner was so popular that a group bestowed on him the title "Patron Saint of Angora" (McSwain 1996). The second development was the National Wool Act of 1954, often cited as the seminal event that brought about the halcyon days of Angora goats and mohair production. Walter L. Pfluger, a rancher from San Angelo, Fred Earwood of Sonora, and Clayton Puckett of Fort Stockton made various trips to Washington, D.C., in attempts to procure a tariff on imported wool and mohair, and they were eventually successful.

Accordingly, the production of wool and mohair skyrocketed. And of course, many shearers were needed to help deliver the valuable product. A 1901 report from the USDA, *Information concerning the Angora Goat*, cited H. T. Fuchs of Tiger Mills as saying that Angora goats had to be sheared twice per year because goats had to endure extreme heat during the summers. More important, if the goats were not sheared twice a year, much mohair could be lost to shedding in the fall (Thompson 1901, 76). This twice-seasonal shearing amplified the need for shearers.

The report further cited that in 1901, fall shearing occurred in September and in the spring during March or April. New "shearing machines" were coming into practice, different from the traditionally used hand, scissor-type shears. The machines by this time were in general use for sheep shearing but not for goat shearing. The machines were said to be more rapid, and the cutting of the animals' skin was minimal. Accordingly the machines were seen as more satisfactory. H. I. Kimball of New Mexico confirmed the rapidity: "I sheared [the goats] myself faster than any hand shearer I ever saw." Another source indicated, "I will say that the clipping machines will work on goats in every respect. I have sheared ten goats in one hour" (Thompson 1901, 77).

According to the report, the shearing was done by "Mexicans in the Southwest who follow the profession." The shearers, who got two cents a head and their board, were able to shear eighty-five to ninety Angora goats per day, but the average was closer to sixty. The report noted that if shearers could shear sheep, they could transition to shearing goats very easily (Thompson 1901, 77).

Easy or not, shearing Angora goats occurred twice a year and could start as early as February and continue until May. Shearers knew this as the long season (*el corte largo*), and the second was the short season (*el corte chiquito*). The latter generally started in mid-July and lasted until mid-September. However, during February and March, it was not uncommon to leave a top of mohair called a cape (*capasete*) on the goat's back to protect it from the ever-unpredictable Texas late winter and early-spring storms.

The technique of shearing Angora goats was almost exactly like that of shearing sheep, except for the last phase. The one major difference was that in shearing sheep, the animal was sheared from the head and shoulders down, while the goat was sheared from its tail down. Said differently, in the final positioning when the shearer was starting at the tail of the animal, the goat was sheared with strokes of the shearing headpiece from the belly to the back. This permits the shearing head-piece to move against the way the locks are attached, which makes the cut much smoother. In essence, if a shearer can shear sheep, he can also shear goats. The skills transitioned to shearing goats very easily.

The sheep-shearing crews in Texas had historically existed for a much longer time than the goat-shearing crews. In other words, the

Angora goats sheared with cape, Kirchner Ranch west of Camp Wood, Texas, 1985. (*Foreground left to right*): Nayo Hernandez, Jonah Carson, and Charles Carson Jr. Photograph from author's collection.

goat-shearing crews developed from the sheep-shearing crews simply because the need to shear goats in large numbers did not come about until the late 1800s. In actuality, the sheep-shearing crews transitioned to being Angora goat shearers. As a matter of fact, it was easier to shear an Angora goat than it was to shear a sheep. Ranchers noted this and always paid less per head for shearing Angora goats. The machinery used for shearing sheep was the same as for shearing goats, although some combs were specialized. The rest of the tools remained basically the same, including the shearing rig.

Whether working with sheep or goats, the shearers were still basically cut from the same cloth, as it were. The Mohair Council of America (n.d.) observed that the men were generally of "Mexican descent" and that coming from West and Southwest Texas, the crews were still nomads who ranged from ranch to ranch with a circuit that generally started in the south and progressed to the north. As in sheep shearing, the captains were the head of the goat-shearing crew and took on its responsibilities.

Similarly, the shearing customs remained largely the same, whether for sheep or goats. One such custom or tradition often seen was familial generations of ranchers having their goats sheared by familial generations of captains and shearers. James Wittenberg of Rocksprings noted this when he told a reporter, "The captain of the crew that shears his goats every spring and fall is the grandson of the man who did the same job for Mr. Wittenberg's grandfather. The shearers are all of Mexican origin" (Reinhold 1985).

In addition, as custom and tradition dictated, the ranchers still rounded up the goats as part of their commitment to the captain, and the captain took over responsibility from there by furnishing the equipment, shearers, boys who picked up the mohair (*laneros*), and the packer (*empacador*) who packed and stomped the mohair into large sacks (Reinhold 1985).

From the late 1940s through the 1970s, business continued to be good in the Nueces Canyon and Edward's Plateau areas of Texas. Mohair was commanding a good price, and goat and sheep prices were also in an upward trend. However, the golden days of the Angora goat and its prized mohair were about to be relegated to history. As much as Angora goat ranchers gained from the Wool Act of 1954, it became a political football. The first major blow to the mohair industry was the removal of the federal government's price support payments. The act was legislatively removed by the Clinton administration when in 1993 Congress voted to phase out the act by 1996, and millions of dollars that had been funneled to ranchers to supplement the income they derived from the sale of wool and mohair ceased.

The act's removal and a general move away from agriculture shrank the nation's and Texas' sheep and goat industry to a fraction of what it once was. In the Edwards Plateau area alone, there were once some six million Angora goats in the peak years of the 1970s. By 2018, there were only an estimated eighty thousand Angoras in the entire United States (Opdyke 1998). The decline was also due to other factors, such as increased production of synthetic materials and changing clothing styles.

Further compounding the problem was the loss of shearers. Professional shearers, some from Mexico, came to Texas to shear the Angora goats twice a year. When the border with Mexico, basically open for decades, was closed, ranchers could be fined for hiring undocumented immigrants. Even in the waning years of generous government mohair subsidies, increased labor costs made it difficult to make a living solely on ranching (Crisp 2017).

The problem of labor shortages was not only a lack of shearers but also a shortage of ranch hands. When interviewed and asked why it was so difficult to make a living raising goats, ranchers spoke of floods, predation, and lack of affordable labor. They felt that for years, the old-time Mexican cowboys, the vaqueros, made goat and sheep ranching possible since they were skilled, loyal, and affordable (Crisp 2017).

Nature also played a role in the decline of the Angora goat industry, not only in the form of unpredictable weather but especially in the form of predation. Predators such as feral hogs are now found in the millions in Texas and other states. They will eat almost anything, including roots, grass, cacti, carrion, and, sadly for the ranchers, deer fawns and kid goats. Feral hog populations have boomed. Five-month-old sows can produce litters of up to eight piglets twice a year (Crisp 2017). Foxes, coyotes, domestic dogs, bobcats, mountain lions, and eagles also add to the predation problem. It was even captured in poetry, as Carlos Culler wrote in "Totem to a Dying Breed":

Clyde killed it with his pickup in 1940
while it was intent on disemboweling a kid
in the middle of the Schleicher County pasture, wingspan: 7'1"
It had taken one or two angoras a week since they had started to
drop in late January and by March he had lost more than twenty of
the flock. (Hill 1994, 186)

Angora billy kids on the Davis Ranch, October 2020. Photograph from author's collection.

Personal accounts paint better the vivid reality of the predator problem. Although speaking of his sheep and not goats, a rancher who resides about four miles west of Barksdale was asked how his herd had been impacted by predators. The rancher recounted that in 2018, he had fifty ewes and raised about that many lambs. He was left with three lambs after the predators, especially the red foxes, finished with them.

But hope springs eternal. In 2019, a rancher from Rocksprings had well over seven hundred nanny goats sheared by a crew out of Del Rio. It looked like the rancher had raised a good percentage of kid goats, and he was going to keep all of the nanny kids to grow his herd. Furthermore, there is presently a bit of an upsurge in Texas, which still ranks at the top in production of sheep and goats. Wool is back in fashion, and sheepskins are all the rage for apparel and decorating in cold climates. And as for mohair, "Wherever there is affluence in the world you will see heavy use of mohair. It is not uncommon for a mohair suit to bring $15,000 in Japan" (Brezosky 2018b).

Registered Angora kids, Davis Ranch, March 2018. Photograph courtesy of Jad Davis.

3

A Legacy of Pride
The Culture of Shearing

Every setting and place where work is done have their own language, jargon, and culture; the shearing industry was no different. The culture of the shearing industry consisted of its ideals, membership, techniques, own language, and various other elements that made up this unique world. One of the most important elements of the culture was its legacy of pride. It has been said that there is dignity in doing one's work well, and indeed just as the mason and the carpenter may be esteemed in their skillful work, so too are the shearers. In an industry that included herders and cowboys, the shearers were considered the "migratory aristocracy" of the trade, as it was considered an "exclusive vocation" (McWilliams 1990, 141).

In the early days, part of that exclusivity and pride was displayed in the way shearers dressed and in the horses they rode:

> The shearers (in groups of twenty to sixty men) would come in, a gay band of Mexicans on prancing horses, decked with wonderful silver-trimmed bridles made of rawhide or braided horsehair, and saddles with high horns, sweeping stirrups, and wide expanse of beautiful, tooled leather. The men themselves were dressed in black broadcloth, high heeled boots, and high crowned wide sombreros which were trimmed with silver-braided bands (McWilliams 1990, 141).

"Most importantly, the shearers performed their work for more than their livelihood; rather, it was their identity, distinguishing them from other Tejanos [Hispanic Texans] who lived on ranches and from those with other trades and skills" (Tijerina 1998, 66).

It must have been quite a scene as these proud shearers arrived at ranches, which could be desolate places. Sarah Blanchard recalled the scene of distinction and pride as she saw the Mexican shearers "galloping up, and it was a time of thrilling excitement" (quoted in Carlson 1982, 58). More recently, Stephany Wilkes expressed the pride she felt in being a shearer when she earned a beginner's certificate from a shearing school in California: "I have never been more proud of anything than the beginner-level sheep shearing certificate I hold in my hands. I may be the first person in my family to graduate from college, and I may have spent seven years earning MS and PhD degrees . . . but those pieces of paper cannot hold a candle to my shearing certificate" (2018, 53).

Just as there is great satisfaction in hitting a baseball with the sweet spot of the bat, or of singing with exultation, such was the feeling when tools were working smoothly and cleanly as a shearer sheared a plump sheep quickly and efficiently. A greater satisfaction was having seasoned, veteran sheep shearers speak well of you as you left the shearing pens or around the campfire at night. In quoting Matthew Crawford, Wilkes said it well:

> A carpenter faces the accusation of his level, an electrician must answer the question of whether the lights are in fact on, a speed shop engine builder sees his results in a quarter-mile time slip. Such standards have a universal validity that is apparent to all, yet the discriminations made by practitioners of an art respond also to aesthetic subtleties that may not be visible to the bystander. Only a fellow journeyman is entitled to say, "nicely done" (Wilkes 2018, 53).

Doing one's work well is also best recognized by the others who do the work themselves. There was great pride among men who could shear two hundred or more goats per day. These were known as *docienteros*, and there were few of them. Those men might also be known as *la espada* (spade), a term derived from card games such as poker. The espada was the shearer who sheared the most animals during the day. The competition to be the espada might continue through an entire shearing season, and it could be brutal. It did not matter if the weather was hot or cold, the pace had to be fast. Stories abounded of men who would compete against each other every day for the whole season. There were stories told in awe of men such as Leon Hidalgo, Manuel "Gugo" Aguero, and Aurelio "Welo" Fernandez. These were men who could consistently shear more than two hundred sheep or goats per day. There was no reason to work so hard except to be the best in the entire crew: pride in vivid display.

Another indicator of the unique culture of an industry is the title that the members of the working crews gave each other. Every crew consisted of men who did the shearing: the *tasinques*. Among the shearers the first to be recognized was *la espada*. The man who sheared the least on a crew was known as *la rata* (the rat). It was never demeaning, since the shearers knew it might be someone who was older, a beginner, or someone who for some reason could not shear very fast. Every shearer received this title at one time or another because, when the shearers were beginners, they were always the ones to shear the least.

The *tesonero* was a shearer who was not necessarily the espada but was known always as a solid shearer. The shearing captain Alejandro Gonzales, known as A. C. Gonzales, from Camp Wood ran his own crew that consisted of as many as twenty shearers. His crew traveled the northern states and sheared from February until the end of June. Don Alejandro bestowed the name "El Rey" (the king) to Macario Aguero Sr. He did so not because Macario was the espada of the crew but because he kept a fast and steady pace the entire season. By the end of the season he was shearing more sheep per day than the shearers who initially exceeded his output. He was a true tesonero and highly admired, as seen by his nickname.

On a negative note, there were shearers who developed a reputation for being *reglistas*. The term denotes "rule," or "ruler," but in shearing circles it was a shearer who too often complained about working conditions, the food, the machinery, the tools, or just about anything else associated with the work. In contrast, shearers who put their head down and went to work were the norm.

Sometimes the shearers assigned particular titles even to the sheep or Angora goats they sheared. For instance, as the shearers sheared a pen full of sheep or goats, eventually the number of unshorn animals dwindled to the last animal, known as *la loba* (loosely translates as "she-wolf"). This was always the animal most difficult to shear, in that it might have matted wool, be very thin or exceptionally large, might have excessive dirt on its back, or possess some of those characteristics combined. It was, in essence, an undesirable animal to shear.

Men who were deft at avoiding the loba were known as *loberos.* They might reduce their speed dramatically to avoid the animal, or they might stop to change out their combs or cutters, or they might go get a drink halfway through shearing their current animal. If the other shearers were not aware, they could be manipulated into shearing the loba. It should be noted that if you did get the loba and it had a lot of dirt on its back, that meant you would have to change out a comb and cutter because the dirt would dull them. Much playful jeering could be heard from shearers if they spotted some lobero purposely trying to avoid the loba. They might joke that the lobero was suddenly in slow motion or note what a coincidence it was that a lobero got thirsty all of a sudden. When a shearer did get the loba, he might yell, "Hey, you all can let your sheep go now; I already got the loba." Or he might exclaim, "This goat didn't bite after all" or "Hey, it doesn't have *pistolas* [pistols] after all."

Another disadvantage to getting the loba was that while the other shearers might already be getting a drink of water, smoking a cigarette, or just plain resting, you were still shearing. However, when in competition, it was good to get the loba; your competitor could not grab another animal to shear, since there were no more left in the pen. The next pen full of animals could not come in until the last animal was sheared. In this case the competitor gained an advantage of one animal more than his opponent. This advantage was called a *cachucha* (loosely translates as "putting a ball cap on someone"). In other words, you now had one more count than your opponent.

Observers have said that the shearers often seemed to be jovial. Upon witnessing the action taking place in a shearing pen, one writer indicated that as the shearing began, there would be sounds of laughing, swearing, and loud calls. The men were further described as "endlessly chattering and singing, laughing, calling out jokes to each other" (Kupper 1945, 152). These descriptions were quite accurate. There were times of hot and difficult work but also of great camaraderie. There were times of sweat and dirt, but at the same time one of the shearers might break out in a great Mexican drinking song by musician José Alfredo Jimenez. Sometimes the day was already long, but there would be one more pen full of goats to shear. The weariness would be alleviated as one of the shearers might yell out, "Pero mañana vamos andar en el baile, tomando cerveza pero bien helada" (Tomorrow we'll be at the dance, drinking really, really cold beer). Another saying often heard started with a *grito* (loud exultation): "No lloro porque te vas; lloro porque no te has ido" (I'm not crying because you are leaving; I'm crying because you haven't left yet). Upon witnessing such a scene during a shearing day in West Texas, one writer described it in a 1954 issue of *West Texas Livestock Weekly*:

> Frequently, the frenzied, yet monotonous sound of the busy machines and crowded sheep pens is punctuated by the whoops of ranch hands as they move unshorn flocks into the corrals. And occasionally those sounds from the shearing floor were a spontaneous rendering of a Spanish song as some sweating worker is suddenly overcome with a memory of a distant wife or sweetheart or perhaps a favorite tavern where air conditioning, leisure, and cold drinks await.

The chatter, singing, and playful quips were part of getting through the day and at the same time enjoying the work. Looking back, I now understand that those were moments of exultation felt when the work was monotonous yet gratifying, when the work was exhausting yet surrounded by camaraderie. Often you heard shearers yelling at one another in a joking fashion. Sometimes they yelled at one particular shearer with whom they *jugavan bien pesado* (engaged in "heavy joking"). Other times they kidded softly as they called each other names such as *suegro* (father-in-law), *cuñado* (brother-in-law), and *lambusco* (brown-noser).

On a personal note, I sometimes in jest would exclaim loudly to my uncle Tano Aguero, who was the captain of the crew, to put in really big *atajos* (pens full of animals to shear) because I needed to make a lot of money to go to college. A shearer named José Castellon would always respond, "Lambusco, vete de una vez!" (Brown-noser, go ahead and leave now!). I still laugh at that memory.

As they kidded in a heavier fashion, a favorite word still heard in many work places is *buey* (ox). Oxen are known for their clumsiness, stupidity, and working without question. Some men bantered so heavily that they cursed at each other, but always in good humor. In some cases cursing was used so often and so heavily that it was once said that God refused to be in the shearing pens because of the foul language. However, there was always one caveat to the kidding. By custom and tradition, shearers could never make those types of comments to people who were to be respected, such as your father, brothers, uncles, or compadres. *Compadre* translates literally in English as "co-father." A centuries-old Spanish tradition was that when one became the godparent of a child, it was a promise to the child's parents that if something were to happen to them, one would raise their child. Respect among compadres was a strongly held tradition in the shearing crews.

In fact, I was the late Tommy Valenzuela's godfather, as I took him to his first communion in the Catholic Church. His father, Tomás Sr., then became my compadre. Tommy became my *ahijado* (godson), and I became his *padrino.* The respect between compadres was to such an extent that even when playing cards together, one compadre did not accept the money from his counterpart when he won a hand. Shearers also would refer to the compadre as *usted* and not *tu.* The first term shows great respect; the other simply acknowledges a person. As done with other persons of great respect, when one's compadre asks something of you, one does not reply, "Que?" (What?); rather, one responds, "Mande" (Give me an order).

There were many other names used in jest or seriousness in the shearing pens. Names such *arrastrado* (slither) referred to persons who were perceived to be lazy. *Desgraciado* (without grace) was a term used for people who could be very mean or sometimes for someone seen as funny. The term could also be used in giving respect to someone who was exceptional, for example, *esta desgraciado para trasquilar* (he is great at shearing). There are other terms that were too vulgar for this type of book, but suffice it to say that most of the time they were used in jest (*jugando pesado*). In retrospect, the shearers who are now remembered at gatherings were men we once worked with, but they were also unique in some fashion or another. Remembering them is like living and working with them once again, and it brings back respect, pride, and joy.

One unique aspect of the culture was in the language that we spoke as shearers. I suppose that many of us in the shearing industry (*trasquila*) did not speak English well at one time or another. Many Hispanic shearers could not speak English fluently, principally because they dropped out of school in the early grades or were from Mexico originally. They communicated in English somewhat, but not in the most correct terms.

Their language was often creative. One shearer once ordered eggs at a restaurant by saying, "Turn them over and take it easy." Another knew that the colloquial term for twins in Spanish was *cuates*. When making a literal translation to English, the word can also mean "shotgun." Upon seeing two kids who seemed to be twins, a shearer asked them if they indeed were shotguns. Another asked for beer as *beeria*. And one asked a waitress to put a quarter in the jukebox and play some music from the *grenudos* ("hairy-headed ones," i.e., the Beatles). Often shearers still sit around and remember those men who supposedly were bilingual, or "bi-language" as one shearer put it. Hearty laughs always follow as they happily remember, never intending to shame; rather, they are simply remembering the way we were.

Even with the Spanish language spoken in la trasquila, there were instances when language variations interfered with one another. For example, a captain who needed laneros went to the streets of a California town to find someone to do the work. He even looked on street corners. He found a few Hispanic young men and asked them if they *juntan lana* (Do you pick up wool?). The young men were apparently *pachucos* who spoke a distinctive lingo/dialect and dressed in white T-shirts and khaki pants. They responded, "Nel no la metemos toda en el pedo." In the pachuco lingo, sometimes known as *Caló*, *lana* means "money," and *juntan* means "Do you save?" So their response was, basically, "No, we spend it all on having fun and drinking." The captain then said in English, "No, I mean would you like to pick up wool for us?" To which the pachucos said, "Chale con ese jale!" (No way with that work!). Many shearers understood and spoke Caló, English, and Spanish. At times all three could be combined during conversations. Many of us as shearers spoke the pachuco dialect. It was spoken in many barrios of Texas, and many of us grew up surrounded by it. Perhaps the most common example of it is the often-used term *ese* (you). Of course, many shearers spoke English fluently, but those who spoke excellent English were often jokingly chided as wanting to be snobby or trying to be too gringo. In truth, being articulate was actually appreciated, but it was simply another reason to have some fun. Those were occasions that indeed made us seem to be jovial and jolly.

The unique culture of shearing was also found around the campfire after a long day's work. We shearers spent many evenings around a campfire when we were literally exhausted and drained after shearing from sunup to sundown during the August days in Texas that often reached over one hundred degrees. An exhausted mind and body brought many things on which to reflect. Thoughts were of days gone by, of days to come, and of people we once knew. Stories abounded.

There was much to learn around those campfires after a long day of shearing. Older shearers told many stories: of times growing up on ranches or in the barrios of Uvalde, Sonora, Camp Wood, San Angelo, or other Texas towns. Many stories were dire. Monica Muñoz Martinez tells of learning from her uncle about the lynching of a Mexican man in Rocksprings; we were told that story, too. Martinez went on to research and write of this tragic event, but she also touches on the meaningful times such as we had around the campfire. She accurately states that many oral traditions of sharing community memories take place within masculine spaces like laborers' campfires (Martinez 2018). Little did we know that culture was being taught to us as we listened to such stories.

We also learned of old traditional stories such as that of *La Llorona*, the spectral woman who had drowned her children in a river and now walked the banks of the river and wailed. We also learned of the young disobedient daughter who danced with a handsome young man, although her parents had not given her permission to attend the dance. Later that night she noticed that the young man had hooves for feet and was indeed the devil. There were lessons to be learned around the campfire.

The stories were not always dire; some were humorous and were often repeated. Such was the story of Leandro Aguero Sr. It was said that at one time he bought a pickup truck on installments from a man in Camp Wood, which was Leandro's hometown. Times got tough and work was sparse, so he could not make the payments on the truck, and inevitably the car dealer came to repossess it. Leandro agreed but asked the dealer to stay out of his yard. He then opened the doors to the pickup and backed the truck up through the gates, which had two large cedar posts on each side. As you can imagine, the doors of the truck were smashed back toward the front of the truck. Leandro then calmly said, "There is your truck and we are even for the payments I did make." The story has been repeated many times since and always gets a smile. Perhaps it remains popular since it was a story of humor, but it was also a lesson in keeping one's dignity.

Often we would be brought back to our reality by someone with a quick wit. One shearer could bring a laugh to us even in tired times. When all was quiet and it was time to go to bed, he would rise, creaky bones and all, and lament, "Cuantas mujeres estaran diciendo, 'si ese hombre fuera sido mi marido'?" (How many women must now be saying, "if only that man had been my husband"?)

After a night's rest, the next morning there would be moments of awe brought about by the sight of watching as many as two thousand sheep and their lambs coming down a low hillside like a wave descending on us. Those large bunches of sheep were called *manadas* (herds). The feeling was somewhat overwhelming, as we shearers knew that all those sheep had to be sheared, one at a time.

In the evening after shearing the herd, there was a different feeling as darkness was coming on and the sheared sheep were set loose from the pen to go back to their lambs. The lambs had been in pens separated from the ewes. Being used to suckling multiple times during the day, they were now starved. Cows can emit a mournful lowing, but the bleating sounds lambs and their mothers make as they try to find each other could never be forgotten. It was a sad and forlorn sound that slowly dissipated as the lambs found their mothers and began to feed and as the herd moved on into the distance. It would now be time once again to sit around the campfire.

Another feature found in the culture of the shearing crews was the use of Spanish sayings, which taught us many lessons and a new manner of communicating culture. Little did I know at the time that the older shearers were teaching us how to act, what to believe, or even how to live through those sayings. Not many of those older shearers were educated or wrote well, so I now know they, too, had heard them from other elders.

One saying was, "Salud, dinero, y amor y tiempo para gozarlos" (Health, money, love, and time and to enjoy them); this was often wished to us as we sneezed. "El que mucho habla poco logra" (He who talks much accomplishes little) was often said when it was time to go back to work. So many sayings that helped form our thoughts and beliefs made up our talk in the shearing settings. It has been written that such lessons are "treasures of a people": "It can be said that sayings are part of cultural treasures of a people because wisdom, wit, philosophy, psychology, and social values of a cultural group are preserved in their sayings. Without a doubt, the sayings of a people are a manifestation of their culture's personality, character, and spirit" (Ballesteros and Ballesteros 1992, v).

Then there were the *puyistas*, men skillful at using double entendre and innuendo to put another person down, and generally in a humorous way. A *puya* was not only double entendre, but it also had a hidden meaning that was imposed on the poor man who did not even know it had just happened. The puyista always won, and the loser was somewhat embarrassed.

Another major part of a shearer's cultural world was the travel involved in doing the work. Elva Treviño Hart (1999) and Saul Sanchez (2014) were field workers who describe themselves as migrants who followed the work to the fields from state to state. Shearers, too, were migrants. Whether two or twenty men, the crews had to move from one ranch to another, simply because that was where the animals were found, perhaps from their homes in Camp Wood to a ranch in Leakey or from Uvalde to Belle Fourche, South Dakota. The shearers were described as arriving on beautiful, prancing horses in the early days (Kupper 1945). In the 1970s, shearers arrived in the back of trucks, on old school buses, or even in their own cars. Though not on a prancing horse, Ruben Balderas once arrived in a brand-new 1969 Pontiac GTO called "The Judge." Rosendo Saiz arrived in a new Dodge Coronet. Before them, Jimmy Balderas Jr. arrived in a new 1963 Ford Fairlane. Different "horses," but still sources of pride. Field workers, as described by Hart and Sanchez, reached a camp and stayed for long periods of time. Shearers, however, moved constantly from one ranch to another. For instance, a captain might shear at a ranch in Montell, Texas, on one day and move his crew all the way to Castle Rock, South Dakota, the next week.

Another distinction from Hart's and Sanchez's migrants was that shearers were almost never accompanied by their families. Since the crews were all men, it would be difficult for families to have any privacy, toilet facilities, or places to sleep or eat. It was a man's world, and bringing families along was often viewed with disdain. Although some shearers did take their families with them, seldom did they stay with the crews on the ranches; rather, they found places to rent in town. An advantage of not having the family along was that the children were able to stay in school, which was often not the case for migrant field workers. However, migrant families often found a profitable advantage if their entire families were able to work, including the children. It was not often that the children of shearers joined them for work. In some instances when families had many sons, fathers and sons worked on the same crews. Often the father might just start his own shearing crew, which included his sons.

As crews moved from ranch to ranch, the shearing captain made contracts. It was understood that the rancher would gather or round up the animals to be sheared and provide pens or corrals in which the shearing was to be done. It was not uncommon for shearing crews to arrive at ranches that were so desolate that no pens were available. However, the rancher and ranch hands soon arrived and would construct pens with steel posts and panels. At times in secluded places even water was not available. In those cases, the rancher often provided a large tank filled with drinking water and transported it on a trailer. It was a lonely sight when shearers arrived at a desolate ranch during the night only to awake the next morning to nothing more than open terrain.

The captain was also responsible for providing travel for the crews. This meant getting his crew and machinery to the ranch. The mode of travel might be in the back of a truck covered with a tarp or on an old school bus, but travel was indeed provided. An inside joke regarding travel was that shearers got to see much of our great country even though it might be from the back of a truck.

However, leaving home on the back of those trucks could have its poignant moments. Josie Aguero Garcia remembered that as a child she often saw her father, Macario Aguero Sr., leave for those unknown, faraway places such as Wyoming, Utah, Montana, California, and South Dakota. She recounted that she still remembered when the big truck from Uvalde came to pick up her father in Camp Wood. He got in the back of the truck and waved to her as they drove away. She in turn ran after the truck crying and not wanting her father to leave. To leave one's family for months on end could not have been easy for the one leaving and assuredly not for the ones staying behind.

Once at the ranch, the captain provided the actual shearing machine/rig, but the shearers provided their own personal tools such as the headpiece, cutters, combs, and other small tools. The shearer's tools were generally kept in toolboxes. Repurposed metal army ammunition boxes were favorites.

Truck for moving workers to the work site, San Angelo, Texas. Russell Lee
Photograph Collection, e_rl_14233_0022, The Dolph Briscoe Center for American
History, The University of Texas at Austin.

Another inside joke was that the crew captain, when contracting men,
would promise to provide room and board. The room in actuality was
whatever was available on the ranch. If shearers were lucky, it might
be a barn or a shed. If not so lucky, they slept under the stars on hard
ground. Some crew captains did provide tents for their men. There were
no bathing facilities, so men were even taught how to wash out of a water
trough designed for use by the animals. Crew members did not wash in
the trough itself; rather, they dipped their hand in the water trough and
scooped water out into their hands and onto their faces. If you washed in
the trough, you would dirty the animal's drinking water. As to restroom
or toilet facilities, none were available. You simply did as bears do.

Board generally consisted of the meat that the rancher provided,
which might be mutton or goat meat. The rest was ordinarily beans,
potatoes, and tortillas. In the early days, the cook (*cocinero*) prepared

the meal on an open fire. Later, trucks or buses were used as "chuck wagons" and might be equipped with butane-fired stoves. When the meal was ready, the men filed through, filled their plates with food, and went outside to eat. In the northern states, goat meat was not available, so the shearers always had mutton. The story is often told of the shearer who, after spending weeks at the ranches, finally went to town to eat a good meal of something besides mutton. Not knowing how to read very well, he ordered lamb chops. When he tasted the meat, he walked out.

The shearers themselves always prepared breakfast. The men filed through the bus, prepared their own eggs, served themselves beans that had been prepared by the cook, grabbed some tortillas and coffee, and then went outside to eat. No tables. The cook prepared lunch and supper. Some captains provided coffee breaks that were taken at about 10:00 a.m. and 4:00 p.m. on most days. The latter break was referred to as a *merienda*. Since it was understood that you would be working late, the merienda was very necessary. This break generally consisted of coffee and something to eat. It might be rice pudding (*atole de arroz*) if you were lucky. It might be a hot taco of tortilla and molasses, or it might be just tortillas left over from lunch. Whatever it was, it was always very welcome.

Shearers taking a *merienda*. Russell Lee Photograph Collection, e_rl_14233r2_0035, The Dolph Briscoe Center for American History, The University of Texas at Austin.

When the crews were shearing close to home, lunch was provided in a number of ways. For instance, when close to their hometown the crews generally went out to the ranch and returned home for the night. In those cases lunch could be provided in various ways. Some captains, such as the late Cresciano "Chano" Falcon of Camp Wood, would provide all three meals. It was a treat to be picked up by his sons and taken to his home for a hot breakfast provided by his wife and daughters. At noon his wife and the girls would take hot food to wherever the crew was working. At dinner the shearers would be brought back to his house for a hot dinner before being taken back to their respective homes for the night. Chano paid slightly less per head sheared, but it was well worth it.

Some captains of small crews provided lunch for shearers, but this was generally prepared on-site at the ranch. One captain always provided the same thing. He would start a small fire at noon and then put a pound of ground beef in a pan; it was very promising. However, when the meat was done, he would then put in a can of peas, corn, or whatever was available on the shelves that day. This sort of ruined the promise. Shearers knew what was in store for lunch if you sheared for that captain. Many other captains did the same, but the fare did differ . . . thankfully.

When shearing on the John Dooley ranch at Laguna, the late crew captain Tano Aguero in some instances would take only tortillas for lunch for the crew. However, he would slaughter a goat early in the morning and put it on the grill for lunch. Lunch was grilled goat meat tacos—incredibly good! In recounting this story, I am often asked how the rancher could afford to give away so many goats. The fact was that many ranchers cross-bred Angora goats with "Spanish" goats (*chivos burdos*). The results were hearty animals that produced little mohair, rendering them almost worthless, but those goats did produce tasty meat. Many times such a breed resulted when the Spanish billy goats would somehow get into the pastures where the Angora nanny goats were kept, or vice versa. But one could generally count on plenty of those cross-bred goats being available. Nowadays no one gives them away; they are too valuable.

Another method of providing food was lunch on your own. The captain honked the truck horn early in the morning in front of the shearer's house. The shearer came out of the house and got in the truck—in the cab if he were lucky—and was taken directly to the ranch. In this case it was understood that breakfast, lunch, and dinner were on your own. Some brought tacos or burritos for lunch, consisting of beans, potatoes, eggs, meat, or whatever was left over from supper. Stories still abound about the unfortunate men whose wives did not get up early in the morning to prepare them a hot breakfast or pack them a lunch. The fare was then something from the grocery or convenience store, and it was either baloney, pressed ham, potted meat, canned Vienna sausages, or something similar. The shearers referred to those types of lunches as *no te levantes honey*, which translates as "don't get up honey" lunches. When men provided their own lunches, the captain might pay a few more cents per head sheared. On a personal note, my mother always packed my favorite lunch for me: bean tacos, a tomato, and a serrano pepper.

One great story that also persisted among the old shearers in Camp Wood is about a shearer name Leonard "Boy" Hernandez III. His friend Evaristo "Buddy" Sena and Boy sheared with Tano Aguero's crew for months at a time. Tano Aguero was known for running a crew where shearers were always going to be camped out at the ranch (*de campo*) so they could start early and be able work late. Many shearers liked that type of crew because they would spend little money on travel, board, or other expenses. Working long hours meant they were going to make good money, too. However, the story goes that they had been working for about three weeks when Boy complained to Buddy at supper, "I wish we would not shear until dark every day." Buddy asked why. "Do you not like working that hard?" To which Boy exclaimed, "No, so I could see what I'm eating for supper!" It was meant to be funny, but the story is also indicative of how late in the day men often worked.

Being away from home was difficult, but shearers seldom wrote their families. Many just did not have the writing skills to do so. However, phone calls were possible. Few families had phones at home, so shearers called someone who did have a phone in their hometown. The message was then given to the wife to be present at the receiving end, fifteen minutes later. In Camp Wood many shearers called the pay phone at Gandy Hidalgo's Texaco station. Someone would pick up the phone, and the shearer would ask that one of Gandy's kids go by the shearer's house and tell the wife, girlfriend, grandmother, or a significant other that the shearer would call back in a while. One of Gandy's kids would go to the house, tell the person being called, and in turn she would go sit by the phone until the shearer called back. The calls were generally to check on the kids or other reasons, such as during holidays.

In cases of emergencies or needs at home, a wife might have to call the shearer. This was done by asking the captain's wife, who also stayed behind in the hometown, if she could reach the crew. The message was in turn given to the captain wherever he was, and the captain would take the shearer to a phone, whether at the rancher's house or in town. Again, this was done only in dire times such as severe illness in the family or news of a death in the family. It was also not uncommon for shearers to miss the birth of a child and have to learn of it by phone.

Attending church was a very rare occasion, since shearing went on continuously for all the days of the week, for all the weeks of the month, and for months on end. The hometowns left behind by the shearers were so bereft of men that on one occasion a man broke into an unoccupied house in the Hispanic part of town and it was quickly known who the culprit was. There was only one person it could be; he was the only Hispanic man left in town.

Shearers did have accidents, such as getting cuts; however, seldom if ever was medical insurance provided. Since most often the shearers were considered subcontractors, they had to provide their own medical insurance; this just did not happen. Shearers simply took their chances. Additionally, while on location, the shearers did not have medical attention except for a first-aid kit. If someone were seriously hurt, a special trip had to be made to the nearest hospital. If the cut were minor, then home remedies (*remedios*) could be the answer. A minor cut could be easily treated with *tecole*, which was a medicinal tarry substance that contained alcohol and an antibiotic but was used to treat sheep or goats that had been cut. Becoming overheated, or what we now know as heatstroke, was treated with mesquite tree leaves soaked in water and placed on the worker's head. If a bad cough persisted, then purple sage (*cenizo*) leaf tea would do the job.

However, serious injuries did occur on the job. For example, Leandro Aguero, "El Borao," once cut his forearm on the rotating edge of a tool sharpener. He was shearing on a ranch in Vance, which was north of Camp Wood. His arm was bleeding profusely, so he was taken to Camp Wood and to his grandmother, Francisca "Wela Kika" Aguero. Known as the healer for the Aguero family, she applied wood-stove soot to the wound to stop the bleeding. Indeed, the bleeding stopped. Then she covered the wound with spider webs to ensure the bleeding would not resume. However, to this day Leandro's arm has the dark coloration of the soot.

As in other work settings, the shearing pens had unique terminology. For instance, shearers used the term *golpe* (a blow) to warn others as sheared animals left the pens. The term functions as a warning when an animal has been loosed, spooked, or was simply running wild and could run into the shearers. Since the shearers worked with their heads down, when they heard the word *golpe*, they knew to immediately look up to see what was happening. It was part of shearers taking care of each other.

Capasete (cape) is a term and procedure used for the protection of recently sheared Angora goats against the cold by leaving the back of the animal unsheared. This left the animal with plenty of mohair on its back for protection against the cold that may come unannounced in Texas. The technique was generally used during the winter or early-spring shearing seasons. Angora goat rancher James Wittenberg said it well: "There are two major enemies for the Angora, predators and the cold" (Reinhold 1985).

Most shearers were ambivalent about using this technique. On the one hand, it was less goat to shear, and on the other, it was cumbersome to revert to a technique that was not common to the shearer's muscle memory and could be quite a nuisance. Since it was outside the shearers' muscle memory, the results could be somewhat funny. Either not enough hair was taken off, resulting in a very shaggy goat, or too much was taken off, resulting in a mostly bald goat. One side could be too long and the other too short.

Another form of protecting goats from the cold was to use the procedure called *al reves* (the opposite way). This basically meant that the goat was to be sheared in the same manner as a sheep. When giving the final touches to the goat, instead of shearing it from its tail to its head, the animal was sheared from its head to its tail. This allowed for shearing "with the grain" of the mohair and thus left much more hair on the animal. Additionally, instead of using the finer "thirteen-tooth comb," the shearer used the much more open "nine-tooth comb," which left much more hair on the goat.

Many sheep ranchers used another shearing procedure, the *desorillo* (tagging). The procedure called for the shearer to shear only the sheep's face, anal area, and udder. Shearing the face allowed the animal to see better as the wool was removed from its eyes. However, many ranchers also sheared the face so that the sheep would not accumulate needle grass on their faces and eyes, which could be injurious to the animals and detract from the quality of the wool. The anal part of the animal being clean of wool prevented fecal matter from attaching to the animal and thus soiling the wool. The udder had to be clean so that lambs could nurse unimpaired when born and during their early growth months.

Shearers would perform the desorillo, since it was done in the out-of-shearing season months. This brought in little income, but it was better than nothing. It usually paid as little as three to ten cents per head, since such a small portion of the animal's body was being sheared. It was also done during the very cold months, so working conditions were unusually harsh. The most negative factor was that the shearers still had to drag one animal at a time to their work station. To make an adequate amount of pay, the shearer had to shear at least two hundred animals per day. It was a lot of work for very little pay, but when there was no other work, you went to the desorillo.

Captains and shearers also often used the term *repepena*. This had to do with going back to ranches after the shearing season to shear those animals that had been left unsheared. This occurred when, for some reason or another, not all the animals had been brought to the ranch pens during shearing time. During the roundup, hundreds of animals could be left behind on large ranches or just a few on small ranches. Seldom did the captain go with the shearers to the repepena; instead, he would send one or two shearers to do the work. Shearing these leftover groups was often a boon to shearers, since they could keep the full price charged to the ranchers and not have to share with the captain.

Finally, another term used in shearing circles was *baratero* (person undercutting pay). This was generally reserved for captains who would go to ranches that were already contracted to another captain. The encroaching captain would offer to shear the rancher's animals for less pay. Since the contracts were usually done by a handshake, a rancher could decide to employ the encroaching captain's crew. As you might guess, barateros were not admired by other captains; however, in the halcyon days of the trasquila, there was so much work that the offended captains just moved on to another rancher.

Another somewhat unique characteristic among the shearing crews was that almost all crew members were awarded nicknames. Names were sometimes given for physical characteristics such as Ben "El Chueco," who walked with a limp; "El Borao" (hazel eyes); "El Guero" (light complexioned); "El Chato" (blunt face); "El Cacheton" (big cheeks); "El Ruco" (the old man); or to someone of small stature, "La Pulga" (the flea). Of course, animal nicknames were used too: "El Borrego" (the ram sheep), "La Liebre" (the jackrabbit), "La Yegua Pinta" (the paint mare), "El Toro" (the bull), "La Copala" (the perch), "La Colmena" (the bee), and "El Macho" (the donkey). Then there was the famous "La Pantalla" (movie screen) given to a fellow who had a huge forehead. The one awarded to the author was "El Profe" (the professor).

Many books and articles on shearing tend to be somewhat romanticized. For instance, one may read that herders, ranch hands, ranchers, and their families saw the time when shearers arrived as the social season: a time to drink, visit, and feast. However, the most inescapable facts about the culture of the shearing industry were the brutal conditions of the work. Shearing work was extremely difficult, meticulous, monotonous, stiflingly hot, and even painful. It was done in barns, sheds, or outdoors under tarps, and the days were long. Sarah Blanchard recalled that the men usually worked from early morning to late in the day, "lasting from daylight until dark" (quoted in Carlson 1982, 58).

An interview with an old-time shearer provides evidence of the difficult and brutal work: "The shearers (*tasinques*) worked in a squatting position, which was painful to their legs and cut off circulation. Another painful part of the shearing was the repetitive squeezing of the scissor blades, which were spring-loaded. Tension on the cutting edges made them very hard to close. The shearers got sore hands, sore arms, and very painful wrists" (Saenz 1999, 14). Another account written in a 1954 issue of *West Texas Livestock Weekly* described the working conditions for a shearing crew in West Texas. The scene in the shearing pen was one that identified the shearers as "almost all . . . of Mexican descent." The men were seen as having "powerful endurance and ability to withstand heat—the stifling, greasy, dusty heat of the shearing pen."

Being able to withstand extreme heat was a quality that shearers had to develop over time, since in the shearing pens the men were surrounded by sheep that were not only smelly but also generated a tremendous amount of body heat. The temperatures were either extremely cold in winter and early spring or notoriously hot in the summer months. "In the shade the thermometer registers one hundred and nine," wrote a Texas rancher (Lehmann 1969, 60). The sheep's wool contained lanolin that covered the men's clothes and made them even hotter. Not only was it suffocatingly hot, but the ambience was one of overwhelming commotion, frustration, and fear. A rancher described the scene in the shearing pens: "Forty or more shearers clicked away with their shears. The temperature was above 90 degrees. I have to contend with a confusion of sounds from about forty pairs of sheep shears and a good many more tongues in a foreign language, and something over seven hundred head of sheep with their bleating" (Lehmann 1969, 60).

Another factor that added to the difficulty of the work was the necessity to dip or spray the sheep with chemicals to delouse the animal or prevent other skin problems. A rancher described the scene when he and his workers became sick as they mixed and used the chemicals. He described the day as unfortunate in that the workers were "wind-up" from the dip that made them so sick (Lehmann 1969, 63). Shearers were sometimes subjected to the same danger if they were "wind-up." It was not uncommon in the 1960s and 1970s for shearers to be covered in the mist from the spray as goats were being treated for lice in an adjacent pen. At the time it felt like a cool mist to their sweating bodies. However, without knowing what chemicals were used in the liquid spray, their safety and health were almost certainly at risk.

In summary, it should be noted that through times of humor, loneliness, exhaustion, or pain, the culture of shearing was both endured and enjoyed. It was difficult work, but it led to esteem. It was lonely, but it provided a good way to make a living. The memories are dying out, and few now tell the stories. It is good to put some of those memories and stories to paper

4

Compensation

THE ACTUAL WORK of shearing sheep and the set of skills needed have changed little over time. The tools have been modernized, but whether a herd of one hundred or one thousand sheep or Angora goats, each animal still has to be sheared individually. However, for every animal sheared the shearer received compensation. Pay was generally from two to six cents per head in the 1700s, and it was always half of what the captain charged the rancher per head. Armando Alonzo notes that in the 1700s, "if for instance the *capitán* negotiated with the sheep owner for five cents a head, he paid the shearer something like three cents per head" (1998, 205).

If you were good at shearing, there was money to be made. In the 1870s "strong, experienced shearers could shear 100 sheep a day, earning $3.00 a day. They were paid three cents a head at the time" (Carlson 1982, 58). Paul Carlson also mentioned the captain paying half of what he charged the rancher: "In the 1870s in the Rio Grande Valley of Texas, normally the prices for shearing a sheep ranged from three to four cents per head. The *capitanes* paid the *tasinques* half of whatever the ranchman paid the *capitán*" (58).

An 1892 federal report found that pay did not differ much in the various US states where sheep were raised. In Montana, shearers were getting eight cents per head; in Texas, five cents; in Arizona, six cents; and in Oregon, seven cents (Salmon 1892). In the northern states pay tended to be somewhat higher because sheep in those states were sheared once per year, while in Texas, ordinarily they were sheared twice per year. One can also safely assume that the captains were earning double what the shearers received. By 1945 the pay was better, and in West Texas the shearer could earn as much as twelve to fifteen cents per head (Kupper 1945). On a personal note, I was paid eleven cents per head when I first began shearing Angora goats. Presently shearers can get as much as five dollars per head.

Pay for shearing often could be an issue. Mention of this was seen at the Tapado hacienda, as the owners considered the cash outlay for shearing to be too high. Charles Harris summarized his description of the shearing work on the latifundios:

> As to payment for shearing at this time, the pay was on a piece meal basis. In 1884, fifty shearers at the Tapado hacienda made a total of 280 pesos. Furthermore, employees were permitted to slaughter a certain number of sheep which averaged 2 per month. However, José Miguel considered the cash outlay too great for shearing. It averaged 1,000 pesos a year although the total revenue for the season had been 56,000 pesos, and the total expense for the season had been 17,000 pesos (1975, 91).

There were instances when the shearers and the captains considered the pay too low. One such disagreement occurred in the 1930s:

> Domingo Garza was the captain of a crew who once sheared for me. In making the contract between us, it was agreed that I was to pay the same price that he was paid elsewhere, no more, no less. But when it came time to settle, he wanted to charge me more that he had been paid by other sheepmen in the neighborhood. I, of course, refused to pay him more than he had received from the nearest neighbor (Maudslay 1951, 119).

A more official disagreement occurred in 1934. Shearers from West Texas became unhappy with their pay and benefits and turned to a shearers' union for help. The contract system was also under scrutiny, as the shearers felt that receiving only half of what was charged the ranchers was not fair:

> Demanding recognition, the union, then 750 strong, called for a wage of six cents a head per sheep sheared, four cents per goat, and two cents

for tagging, prices they felt were reasonable based upon the 100 to 150 sheep that good shearers could turn out daily (remember that twice this amount would have to be paid to the *capitán*). The ranchers however, balked at the demands. On January 4, 1934, ranchmen owning property in twenty-five West Texas counties established a maximum of eight cents a head for shearing sheep, five cents for goats, and two cents for tagging (remember that only half went to the *tasinques*). Another argument of the *tasinques* was that they seemingly sacrificed themselves to provide captains with good homes, automobiles, and plenty of money. On February 15, 1934, the special organizer spoke… before some 400 *tasinques* (De León 2015, 117).

The strike was not successful, as ranchers hired tasinques from Mexico and broke the strike. The practice of reganche also came under fire as in 1922, when the Sheep and Goat Raisers Association of Texas agreed that "they would abolish the *reganche* system. Ranchers were apparently fed up with advancing money to shearing captains. Shearing captains in turn gave advanced pay to their shearers in order to help them during shearing off-season hard times" (McSwain 1996, 202).

Advanced pay was important for shearers. Since the work was seasonal, shearers often had to have pay in advance to provide for their families in the off-season. The formal term used for such pay was *enganche*, but the most widely known and used term was *reganche*. *Enganche* loosely translates to "hooked." In many instances the captain too would go to ranchers and obtain partial pay in advance. Those funds were then deducted from the payment made by the rancher when the shearing was completed. Reganche for the shearers typically came in October, November, December, and January since those were the months when there was little other work to do.

Migrant field work could also be an option to earn income. Following the beet work, picking cotton and other field work were generally available, but it always meant much travel and involved uprooting the entire family. The children often had to be taken out of school, and the entire family was sure to live in very poor housing. It was fine for the shearers to live in barns or sleep outdoors, but the entire family having to do so was an entirely different proposition. Shearers did not often do field work; after all, there was much more dignity in shearing.

An example of the importance of reganche in the off-season can be seen in the area near Camp Wood. At that time shearers ordinarily depended on income from cutting cedar or building fences, but it was very difficult work during November through January, which is hunting season in Texas. Ranchers leased out their land to deer hunters to generate another valuable source of income. Cedar cutters or fence builders were not allowed on the ranches because of the danger of being shot or because deer hunters complained that the noise from workers scared off their game. Thus, there was no other work for shearers, and the captain ensured he would have shearers under contract by advancing them pay.

At Christmas, when the shearers needed to provide holiday clothes, gifts, and fare for their families, the captain might advance sums of three hundred to five hundred dollars. Santiago Uriegas Jr. of San Angelo recalls that his father told stories of reganche at Christmas. Uriegas Sr. said that most people were poor, but the shearers always had presents for their families because of the reganche provided by the captains. When they received the money, the shearers would buy clothes for the kids and apples and oranges for presents (Whittley 2002).

However, for the shearers there was a reckoning. Once they started shearing, it would be a good amount of time before they made any money since they would be paying off the reganche debt. For the captain, reganche was advantageous and risky at the same time: advantageous in that the captain was somewhat assured that he would have his men under contract, called *reganchados,* and ready for the upcoming season; risky in that the men might decide at the last minute not to be found when it was time to shear, or they might decide to go with some other captain to whom they did not owe any money. Again, the contracts were simply handshakes and could easily be broken. In either case, those shearers who broke the verbal contracts might develop a bad reputation and not be able to receive reganche from any other captain when needed.

The colloquial term used when a man who could not be found at the time to begin work was that the shearer *le corrio al capitán* (he ran from the captain). This did not happen often, since most shearers fiercely protected their reputations. In South Dakota a shearer once ran from the captain, but the captain knew where he was staying. The shearer became indignant and threatened the captain, who promptly pulled his gun and shot the man. No fatality resulted, but the captain now had a reputation, too. In an interview, an old Uvalde captain talked of the risk shearing captains took when providing advanced pay. Juan Santos reflected on the huge losses that could run into the thousands of dollars given in reganche to shearers who might not keep their word. Santos said such losses were inevitable (Fenly 1967).

Seemingly, once the reganche debt was paid to the captain, the tasinque made nothing but profit. However, the debt could be ongoing because while shearing away from home, the shearer had to send money to his family and had to ask the captain to send the money. It was a very dignified way for men to care for their families, since they sometimes had to be gone for up to five months. It was sometimes very difficult for the shearer to finally catch up on his debt to the captain. If, for instance, the shearer owed two hundred dollars of advanced pay and was sending home another three hundred dollars, then the debt persisted until enough sheep could be sheared.

There were times when shearers would also ask the captain for money when they had some time off due to bad weather or while moving from

Shearers at their favorite bar during a day off in San Angelo. Russell Lee Photograph Collection, e_rl_14233_0047, The Dolph Briscoe Center for American History, The University of Texas at Austin.

one ranch to another. The shearer might ask for ten dollars for the day to eat in town or rent a place to stay (usually with three or four other men). In this case the shearer was said to be "taking out money" (*sacando dinero*). For many men, the time off was a chance to unwind, and one of the best ways to do it was to go to a bar for a cold beer or two.

In conversation with shearers, they would invariably tell you of their favorite bars in the cities they visited. Old shearers in Camp Wood would usually tell you that the Old Back Bar in downtown Belle Fourche, South Dakota, was one of their favorite hangouts. The Hank Williams songs were familiar, and the beer was cold. The Five Mile Bar, some five miles outside Belle Fourche, was also a well-recognized hangout.

Interestingly, one of the most common things talked about during the breaks was shearing. Even after working many days, when getting together for relaxation, the men spoke of shearing. It was not the typical "around the campfire" discussions, but often they spoke of how many so-and-so could shear, and they often spoke in awe of men who were great shearers. Dionisio Sifuentes Jr., "El Ruco," recalls one such discussion at the Old Back Bar when he walked up to the shearers at the bar and told them to stop for a minute so he could pick up the wool, since it was now filling up the place. The shearers did not think that was very funny.

Manuel "Paipe" Aguero used to tell the story that at one time he and Tomás Valenzuela, "El Toro," were drinking beer with El Ruco at the Five Mile Bar. El Ruco had downed a few beers already and was talking about shearing—of course. He was speaking of a day when he had sheared more than two hundred sheep by 5:00 p.m. He said that he could have sheared more, but there were no more for that day. He would turn to Paipe and say, "Isn't that right, Paipe? You were there." Paipe would say, "Oh yes, I was there." To make a long story short, after every tale, El Ruco would buy another round for all three men, and Paipe and Tomás would both say, "Yes, we were both there." At a certain point El Ruco realized what he was doing and said, "Hey, wait a minute; it's you guys' turn to buy a beer." To which Paipe and Tomás said, "No, no, keep shearing; we don't want to shear right now; we're doing fine here." Any old shearer could tell you many of those types of stories.

The determination of just how much shearers earned was made by keeping a daily count of the number of sheep sheared. Shearers arrived at their daily total by counting the number of tokens they accumulated during the day. After each animal was sheared, the lanero picking up the wool would give the shearer a token that he promptly put in his pocket. The token itself could be a washer, coin, pebble, or even coins from Mexico. Some captains created their own distinctive tokens. A rancher from Sonora told of finding a token that had the words "good for fifty sheep" printed on it. He wondered how that token could have been used. The answer was that in such a case and typically at noon, the shearers might have so many tokens in their pockets that it became quite cumbersome to carry all of them as the day progressed. So the shearer could count out fifty tokens at noon and replace them with the "good for fifty sheep" token.

The daily count was reported to the captain in many different settings, but typically the captain asked each man how many he had sheared that day as everyone sat around eating supper. The captain wrote down in his ledger the number sheared by each man. It might go something like this: "Beto, *cuantas* [how many]?" "163." "Gugo, *cuantas?*" "195." Each man would give his total when his name was called. This could also be a time of commenting in recognition of a shearer's impressive total with expressions such as *que sorgita* (what a great one), always laughingly and in good jest. On one occasion, a man known as "Primo Beto" who was the rata of the crew would joke to the captain, "*Despues le mando una notita*" (I'll send you a little note later). Again, another moment of being jovial.

At the end of the season the captain and the shearer summed up or totaled out, *arreglaban*. The captain totaled the number of sheep the shearer had sheared during the entire season. The season's count was arrived at by totaling up the number of sheep the man sheared on a daily basis. As the total sheep sheared in one season was reached, the captain then summed up how much money the shearer had sent home, how much he had received in reganche, and how much he had taken out during days off. The total owed was subtracted from the amount earned. The money left over was how much the shearer had made after debt (*alcansó*). It was not uncommon for shearers to owe more than they had made. It could be a very difficult cycle as the debt was carried over to the next season.

A factor that was rarely considered in the method of payment was retirement savings. In most instances, for payroll reasons the captains would simply designate their workers as contract workers; that is, each shearer was self-employed and thus responsible for saving for his own retirement and Social Security payments and benefits. There were not many instances when shearers actually ever paid into their Social Security accounts. Many times, old shearers who could no longer shear found themselves with no retirement benefits. Of course, there are records of captains indeed taking Social Security payments from shearers and paying their share of the benefits into their respective accounts.

Finally, if one were to ask shearers why they sheared, they would probably reply in jest, "Porque por dinero baila el chango" (Because the monkey dances for money). However, when I posed the question to the three shearers interviewed for this book, they all gave the same reply: "It was a good, honest way to make a living."

5

Las Máquinas
The Crews

THE LATE MANUEL TALAVERA of Uvalde was born on February 2, 1928. I spoke with eighty-nine-year-old Manuel in the spring of 2018 regarding a photograph of the Moises Reyes crew taken in Utah in 1946 when Talavera was eighteen years old. He is the towheaded young man on the top row, second from the right. He was not a shearer but had accompanied the Moises Reyes crew of Uvalde as a lanero. Sadly Manuel Talavera died on August 9, 2018; I was indeed fortunate to have met and spoken with this kind gentleman, who gave me great insight into the photograph.

I obtained the photo from my aunt Virginia Aguero Valenzuela, who possessed it because our uncle Tano Aguero was shearing with the crew. According to what Tano Aguero told Virginia, everyone in the crew had been given a copy of the photo at the end of the shearing season. Uncle Tano Aguero is the fifth man from the right with the train engineer's hat. Manuel Talavera identified the man in the hat (sixth from the right) as Ben Perez, nicknamed Ben "El Chueco," who was one of the best, if not the best, shearer to ever come out of Uvalde.

Manuel identified Porfirio Rodriguez, the empacador for the crew, at the top right. Matilde Jimenez, another empacador, is next. To his right is the captain of the crew, Moises Reyes, who has a cigarette in his mouth. The only man sitting in the picture is Inez Reyes, Moises's brother. The names of the other men were listed on the back of the picture but were not identified by position: Roberto Nevarez, Willie Hernandez, Santos Olivarez, Cuco Reyes, Manuel Ortiz, Jabiel Reyes, Adolfo Vara, Jabiel

The Moises Reyes crew of Uvalde, Texas, in Utah, 1946. Photograph courtesy of Virginia Aguero Valenzuela.

Vara, Ramon Reyes, Frito Rodriquez, Toño el Gordo, Poldo Flores, Beto el Sapo, Santos Bustamantes, Manuel Carabajal, and Porfirio Rodriguez.

This is one of the few clear and vivid photographs of men in one of the typical crews that sheared thousands of sheep and goats in Texas and northern states. The crews were better known as *la máquina* (the machine) or *la companía* (the company), for example, "*la máquina* de Moises Reyes" or "*la companía* de Frank Hidalgo." The crews consisted of two, three, or as many as thirty-two men. In the early days of shearing the crew could consist of as many as sixty men.

There were many crews throughout Texas, documented at the request of the Texas Sheep and Goat Raisers Association as they developed a list of shearing crews to strengthen their argument to secure federal funding for sheep and Angora goat ranchers. The shearing crews on the list were identified by the name of the captain of the crew. It should be noted that almost in all cases the captain also owned the crew (Whittley 2002).

Sandy Whittley listed four captains from Brackettville, including Richard Peña and Gregorio Sandoval. The city of Brady showed four, including Lupe Zapata. Camp Wood had six captains listed, including Manuel and Tano Aguero, Leonard "Boy" Hernandez, and Gandy

Hidalgo. Fredericksburg had Perry Hohenberger listed as the captain. Other cities included were Del Rio, Eden, Eldorado, Fort Stockton, Gatesville, Goldthwaite, Junction, Lometa, Menard, Mineral Wells, Missouri City, Mullin, Ozona, and Rocksprings. The list became extremely important as the legislative argument was developed to show how many people and communities would be impacted if federal funds were not granted.

Rocksprings has been a community strong in shearers. Barbara Perkins (2018), in writing of the F5 tornado that hit Rocksprings in 1927, listed Hispanic families that were injured or who had members killed by the storm. She also listed their occupations and perhaps inadvertently captured an early history of shearing in Rocksprings. The men listed were the Carabajal family, including Victoriano, who was a shearer; Manuel Lozano Davalos, Rafael Jimenez, and Remijio Palacios were also listed as shearers.

More currently, Sandy Whittley (2002) also listed twelve captains from Rocksprings, including Eddie Franco Sr., Paco Ramirez, Rene Galindo, and Belio Villarreal. San Angelo, Santa Anna, Sonora, and Sterling City were included in the list, along with San Saba, which had twelve captains listed. Uvalde listed nine captains, including Frank Gonzales, Johnny Lara, and Alex Reyes. The list is long; however, it was only a sampling of the many captains who worked over time. Those who are listed are the crews of the 1990s, but there were many others before them.

As early as the 1930s and through the 1980s, Uvalde was known as the epicenter for large crews that traveled in Texas and to *el norte* (north). Crews from Uvalde such as those of Juan B. Reyes, Lidio Reyes, Moises Reyes, Fermin Reyes, Fito Santos, Andalecio Gonzales, Alejandro Gonzales, and Nick Flores, were well-known and might consist of as many as thirty-two shearers. Forms that were filled out for the Shearers Convention 2002 held in Uvalde not only listed the captains but also the fact that their crews sheared as many as one hundred thousand sheep each per season.

Shearer Guillermo Quirova of Uvalde sent in a letter with his personal story for the convention and indicated he was born in 1923 and began working as a lanero at the age of eight, earning fifteen dollars a month. He went on to become a shearer and worked on the crews of Juan

Reyes, Alejandro Gonzales, Cruz Santos, Fernando Gallardo, Rito Perez, Poncho Castro, Pedro Castro, Jose Valle, and Sam Castro. The letter is important historically because it identified these crews.

Many more captains were listed in a research paper, *Sheep Shearing Contractors of Uvalde County and Their Tokens*. Captains from Uvalde mentioned in the paper were Francisco Castro, Pedro Castro, Ben G. Perez, Fermin Reyes, Juan Santos, J. V. Santos and Sons, and Fernando Gallardo (Albin 2002). It should be noted that there were many more crews and captains in Uvalde, but not all could be listed in this book.

Florence Fenly provided in 1967 a good description of one of the pioneer Uvalde shearing crew captains, Juan Reyes. He was born on March 30, 1887, and was eighty years old at the time he was interviewed. Reyes started his shearing crew in 1917; however, he had begun his work as a shearer on other crews such as those of Manuel Aguilera and Juan Gonzales. In the year he started his crew, Juan Reyes had actually been drafted to fight in World War I; however, since he was a worker doing "vital work for the nation," he did not go to war after all. He married Clara Treviño of Brackettville in 1912, and they had two sons, Lidio and Cuco.

Reyes remembered shearing as many as one hundred thousand sheep in Colorado, Utah, and Montana with crews that included thirty-two shearers; he made those runs for twenty-five years. Reyes recounted that in the early years ranchers paid ten cents per head in Colorado and the crew sheared about sixty thousand sheep. Captains paid the shearers half of what they charged the rancher and provided them with food. The crew consisted of the shearers, four laneros, two *amaradores* (who tied the fleeces), and two empacadors. They did provide tents, stoves, and cots for the men. Reyes also remembered providing reganche.

Juan Reyes's son Lidio went on to form his own crew at the age of twenty. However, before then he was an amarador and a *tecolero* (applicator of worming medicine) and became a shearer at the age of seventeen. He learned the business from his father and become a contractor and shearing captain who sheared some of the larger flocks in the country, such as those at the Lee Aldwell ranches, the Sayer Cattle Company of Texas, the G. W. and J. C. Cunningham Ranch of Fort Stockton, and Fields Brothers of Sonora (Fenly 1967).

Not all crews had large numbers of shearers. Some were small crews and were not listed by Whittley but still worked for many years. For instance, crews from Camp Wood might consist of as few as two shearers, such as the Ben Carabajal crew, or three, such as the Chon Barron crew. Shearing crews from Camp Wood tended to be smaller because they consisted of mostly family members. Some of those families, such as the Hidalgos, De Leons (Javiel and Guadalupe), Falcons, Valenzuelas, Nevarezes, Carabajals, Gonzaleses, Ruizes, and Agueros, came to the Nueces River Valley between 1910 and 1925: certainly not as early as the Spaniards who, in 1762–67, established and later abandoned the missions of Nuestra Señora de la Candelaria in Montell and San Lorenzo de la Santa Cruz in Camp Wood, but early enough to become part of the people who established the communities of Camp Wood and Montell. Those Hispanic pioneer families came and stayed because initially they made a living by cutting cedar and firewood for the Uvalde and Northern Railroad Company that hauled cedar from Camp Wood and surrounding areas to Uvalde and then to other parts of the United States. The Northern Railroad company employed as many as two hundred cedar cutters (Roberts 2018).

Some of those pioneers also came as vaqueros to work on ranches, such as Manuel Aguero Sr., who worked on the Arthur Beck and Mamie Powers ranches west of Barksdale. As the demand for cedar wood declined, the pioneers had to find other work. Additionally, as the families on the ranches grew in size, they had to move to town to find work for all their young men. The timing was opportune, as the numbers of sheep and goats increased dramatically in the area, and the demand for shearers came with it. The pioneer men and their boys turned to shearing. For the Camp Wood area, this was the beginning of a shearing tradition that lasted almost ninety years.

As stated earlier, the smaller crews created in the Camp Wood area were made up mostly of family members. Some examples include Juan Falcon, Manuel Hidalgo, Manuel Aguero, Polo Nevarez, Javiel De Leon, and Guadalupe De Leon and their sons. Through them, the sons and grandsons of those sons learned the skills and culture of the trasquila.

Early writing about shearing introduced and described the titles of shearing crew members. Those titles never changed from the 1700s until the industry faded. There has always been a shearing captain, the shearer, the boy picking up the wool or mohair, the boy applying worm medicine, the packer, and the cook, described in this excerpt:

> Besides the *tasinques* who formed the backbone of the crew, the team required other members. The crew always had a *cocinero*. There was also an *amolador*, whose job it was to hone the blades for the *tasinques*. One or two *laneros*, depending on the size of the rig, gathered the wool and issued the *tasinque* a token (cheque) for each sheep sheared. The *laneros* would hand the wool to the *empacador*, usually a heavy-set man, who had a four-pod contraption about eight or nine feet high from which he hung a big and heavy burlap sack (*las sacas*). It was the man's job to get inside the bag and pack down the wool (Guerrero 1991, 44).

Some crews still shear small herds such as the three-man crew who is headed by Chavel Sanchez of Camp Wood. Another example is Stephany Wilkes of California, who is a one-woman crew, but there are few who have continued the work to the present day. However, in the halcyon days of shearing, the crews consisted of many team members, and perhaps the most important member of the crew was the captain (*capitán*). Early writings describe the role: "Before leaving Mexico, each band elected one of their number a captain, who enforced obedience, maintained order, and made contracts with the sheep owner regarding time of shearing, the price to be paid and the food and the accommodation to be furnished" (Lehmann 1969, 55). The captain was often described as the man who recruited the shearers, established the contracts for times to be at ranches, arranged payment for himself and the shearers, transported the men and machinery, scheduled meals and breaks, and enforced discipline.

Such early descriptions of the captain held true for many years. Indeed, in the 1960s through the early 1990s, the personnel on the shearing crews were most often led by the captains, who were men who had to be a "jack of all trades." Typically, one would end the phrase above with "and master of none," but that would be inaccurate in this case since, by necessity, the captain had to be adept at all the tasks of the crew. First of all, as *contratista* (contractor), he worked with ranchers to negotiate a contract, sealed by a handshake, to shear their sheep and/or goats. Once arranging the contract with a rancher, it was not uncommon for the same captain to shear for that rancher for many years, and often those contracts continued for various family generations of the captain and the rancher. For instance, Javiel De Leon sheared for Dolph Briscoe, ex-governor of Texas, for many years. Javiel's sons continued to do so after Javiel passed away.

The captain not only contracted the work for his shearers, but he hired and assembled all the crew members. He then had to transport the men to the ranches where they were to work. Thus, he provided the transportation for the men unless a shearer took his own vehicle, which was seldom the case. Once at their destination, it was also the responsibility of the captain to provide room and board for the crew, except that each crew member provided his own bedroll.

The captain provided the major tools for the men. The trucks, the ingenio, later called la máquina (shearing machine), and all its parts and maintenance were the captain's responsibility. In later years, the captain provided the electric generator and electric motors that powered the shearers' hand-held headpieces. The captain also provided gasoline for the trucks, engines, and all the lubricants/oil for the tools. However, it was the responsibility of the individual shearer to provide his own shearing headpiece, cutters, combs, specialized screwdriver, and other smaller tools.

The captain was also in charge of all financial matters beyond the contract, including providing reganche. He handled all bookkeeping matters, including keeping count of the animals sheared by individual shearers, making payment during the shearing season, and making final settlement at the end of a season. He was head of transportation, contracting, facilities, equipment, provision of food and water, and discipline.

The crew could not exist without the shearers (*tasinques*), who did the actual removing of the wool and/or mohair from the animals. Thus an entire chapter of this book is dedicated to them.

Another important member of the crew was the cook (*cocinero*). The work was hard, so the food had to be of good quality. As V. W. Lehmann notes, "The work was hard, lasting from daylight until dark; the food supply was simple, consisting of meat, bread, beans, rice, and coffee" (1969, 57). Often thought of as the most important position on a crew, the cook was integral to its smooth functioning. Though usually a man, in some instances the cook was a woman. A good example is Francisca Aguero, who managed to cook the beans, tortillas, and meat that the men ate on a daily basis. She cooked on an open fire for as many as twelve shearers and the other members of the crew. A fine poetic description of such a cook was provided in 2004:

> **A ghost figure at the stove, I see her**
> **Moving from end to end to stir**
> **Kettles and pots and pans full**
> **To give sustenance to us all. (Garcia 2004, 66)**

Initially all cocineros cooked on an open fire. Then they progressed to cooking on a stove, usually fueled from a butane or propane tank. The stoves were installed in chuck wagon–type trucks. These were the larger truck models outfitted with flat beds, large rails on each side, and covered with tarps. The trucks served as mobile kitchens, were used to carry the crew's bedrolls, and often were utilized to transport the men when moving from ranch to ranch. Old school buses converted to mobile kitchens came into use in the late 1960s and early 1970s. The cook provided the three meals for the crew if they were to be de campo at the ranch. They would also provide the coffee and snack for the merienda. Employed by the captain on a pay-per-day basis, the cooks were generally respected but could be unpopular if they were not adept at their trade. Shearers often asked who was to be the cook before they agreed to work for a captain.

When the tortillas ran out before all the men were served, it was said that a home run had been hit; cooks did not like that term. However, one of the favorite items some cooks could prepare was the *pan de campo* (camp bread), which was a delicious baked bread. It was especially delicious when cooked in Dutch ovens over mesquite wood coals. Men such as Nicho Sifuentes and Chon Falcon, both of Camp Wood, were famous for their pan de campo.

Back in the shearing pen, another crew member was the *lanero*. This was generally a young man whose primary and most important task was to be on hand when an animal was sheared. The lanero then picked up the wool or mohair from that animal and took it to a table located in front of the *empacadora* (packing-machine contraption) so that the

El cocinero. Russell Lee Photograph Collection, e_rl_14233r2_0037, The Dolph Briscoe Center for American History, The University of Texas at Austin.

empacador could pack it into the large sacks that would eventually be taken to the wool warehouse to be sold.

The second major task for the lanero was responsibility for handing the shearer his token for each animal sheared. The lanero's pockets had to be full of tokens for the task to be done quickly. If for some reason the lanero was not quick enough to be on hand when the shearer released an animal and wanted his check/token, the loud exclamation would be, "Bola, lanero!" (loosely, "Token, wool-boy!"). It was hard, continuous work, and the young men could not slow down or they would hear from the shearers the dreaded "Bola, lanero." The shearer could not slow down since there was money to be made; or slowing down might mean that the competitor to the espada could catch up to him.

Good laneros seldom got behind in their work of handing out the token and picking up the wool or mohair; if they did, they would owe the shearer a token. In such cases the shearer might yell out, "Me debes una" (You owe me one). The lanero would have to keep track of this and hand the shearer double the next time. Some shearers could be impatient. If the lanero was not quick enough to pick up the wool or mohair from the shearer's station, it was not uncommon for the shearer to just kick it out of the way. Where crews were large, there were generally shearers lined up on both sides of the shearing rig with one lanero for each side, since one would not be enough to handle all shearers.

In the morning before shearing started, it was also the lanero's job to fill up the large water cans from which the men drank during breaks. Another responsibility was watering down the pen so that less dust would be created. If water from a hose was available, the job was relatively easy. If there was no hose, water had to be carried in pails from a nearby water trough. Breathing that dust in was not good for shearers, but saving wool or mohair was another reason for not having a dusty pen; the mohair or wool that tended to litter the shearing pen would not become overly dust-covered and thus less valuable or wasted. The ranchers made sure that the captains pushed the laneros to keep the pen moist.

When the engine of the shearing rig ran out of gas, it was the lanero's job to fill it up. If the engine indeed ran out of gas, that typically meant the laneros had not done their job. The crews generally carried the gasoline in cans or fifty-five-gallon drums. However, if those ever ran out of gas, the lanero would then need to perform the dreaded task of extracting gas from the tanks of the trucks. This was usually done by inserting a hose into the gas tank and then sucking on the hose until the gas started flowing into a waiting can. However, the task was unpopular, since if they were not quick enough, the laneros could take gasoline into their mouths, which was not pleasant.

One of the simplest jobs but another menial duty for the lanero was to fill up an oil can for each shearer. The shearers had to have oil on hand to spread it over the headpiece's comb and cutter. Much friction is created as the cutter moves over the comb, and if it is not lubricated, this causes the headpiece to overheat. The headpiece was constantly hot, so overheating could be a real problem for the shearer's hand. When the laneros were too hurried or shearers criticized them, a trick would get them quick revenge. The lanero could coat the entire headpiece with oil so that when the shearer grabbed it, it was oily and slippery and he had to take time to clean it. That usually got a laugh from the other shearers, but it was always in good fun.

Watching and caring for the shearing pen corners (*cuidar las esquinas*) was a part of the job laneros dreaded. This was to ensure that the animals, especially kid goats and lambs, did not collapse in the corners of the shearing pens and go under the rest of the animals. The collapsed animals were sure to suffocate if they were not gotten to their feet immediately. If the animal was already down and gasping for breath, the lanero would move the two front legs up and down quickly. This usually brought the animal back to life. Added pressure to an already busy job!

Once the lanero got the wool or mohair to the table, another man's job came into play. It was the task of the packer (*empacador*) to get the wool ready for hauling. The wool and mohair were packed into large burlap sacks that were as long as seven feet. In early days it was done by hand and foot. The packers placed the wool fleeces into the burlap sacks, then got into the sack and tramped the wool down with their feet. When the sack was full, they would remove the sack from the empacadora, sew the open end, remove it from the contraption, and roll it aside. They could easily fill more than fifty sacks in one day if the crews had ten or more men (Guerrero 1991, 44).

Also, Helen Hunt Jackson stated in the 1870s:

> It was warm work. The dust from the fleeces and trampling feet filled
> the air. As the sun rose higher in the sky sweat poured off the men's
> faces. After the bag of fleeces was half full, the packer stands in it,
> jumping with his full weight on the wool, as he throws in the fleeces to
> compress them as much as possible (Wentworth 1948, 112.)

In late 1960s and early 1970s, the empacadora was modernized. It now consisted of a large cylinder with a hydraulic rod that pushed the wool into the sacks. There is also now a new method in which the wool is packed into large square sacks that are baled by a machine, which makes the sacks much easier to handle.

Another essential crew member who could be a very popular person—or not—was the *amolador*, who sharpened the combs and cutters for the shearers. This was in most cases the captain; however, large crews sometimes had a man who was hired specifically to do the sharpening. Ordinarily the tools were sharpened early in the morning before the daily shearing started or late in the evening before the next day's work.

Young man "tromping" the mohair into the sack on a ranch near Sonora, October 2020. Photograph from author's collection.

However, the sharpening also went on during the day as needed. In the 1940s and 1950s on some crews, each individual shearer was responsible for sharpening his own tools.

Crew captain Catarino Valenzuela Jr. sharpening shearing tools at a ranch east of Rocksprings, Texas, April 2019. Photograph from author's collection.

The metal sharpening device was known as a *moyejón*, which consisted of a large metal disc that had to be rotated very fast to sharpen the tools. Originally the sharpener was rotated by a hand crank. In later years it was attached to a rod with a pulley driven by a belt that was in turn attached to the gas engine that drove the shearing belts. In more current years, and presently, the sharpener is attached to an electric motor. In all cases, the amolador had to be very skillful and careful to

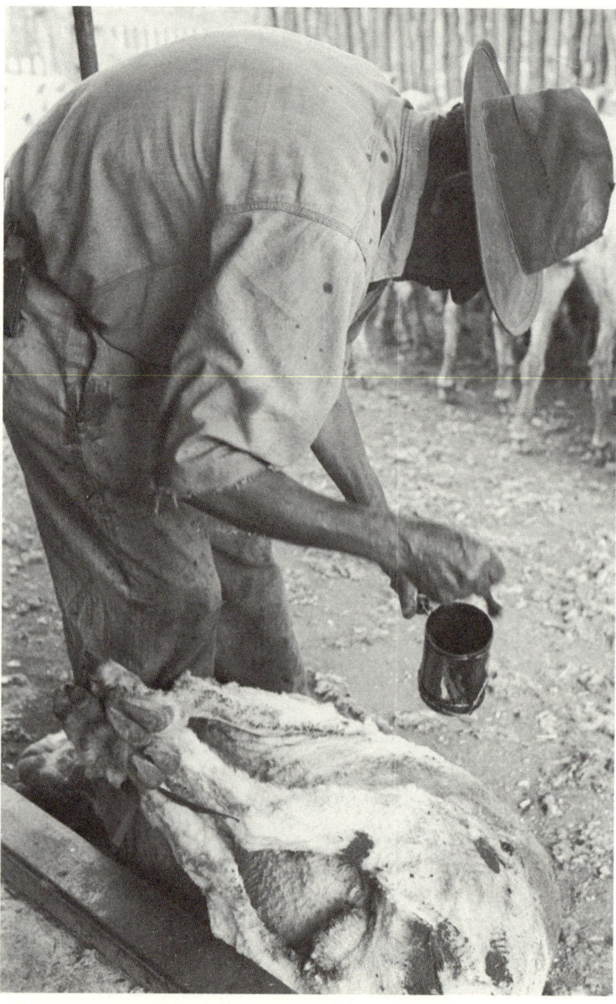

El tecolero. Russell Lee Photograph Collection, e_rl_14233r2_0024, The Dolph Briscoe Center for American History, The University of Texas at Austin.

do the work correctly. If the tools were pushed too hard, they would wear out too quickly. If pushed too lightly, the tools would not be sharp enough to cut the fiber. This was very important since, if not sharp, the tools made the work very slow, tedious, and next to impossible to do.

Needless to say, a good amolador was very much appreciated and praised. A bad one generally did not last and was privately cursed. Pay for the amolador could be a daily wage or an extra few cents for every sheep or goat he sheared. For instance, he might get thirty cents per head sheared rather than the standard twenty-five cents. This was not a very good deal, since the amolador could not shear many animals if he was too busy during the day sharpening tools for others. However, the best deal to be made was to be paid per head on the sheep sheared by all of the shearers. For instance, the amolador might receive five cents per head for the total sheared in one day by the entire crew. That amount, along with the number he sheared in one day, could be a tidy sum.

An additional crew member who disappeared from shearing crews over time was the *tecolero*: "Hovering nearby were young boys who applied a tarry mixture to the many nicks on the animal. If this was not done, blow flies would lay their eggs in the open wounds, which in a few days would be covered with a mass of worms feeding on the sheep's flesh" (Harris 1975, 33). The tecolero was indeed vital to a shearing crew, but more so to the rancher. The name comes from the medicine applied to the wound of the animal, the tecole, which consisted of a thick mixture of tar and some form of alcohol that would cover the wound completely. Very often during the day you could hear the shearers exclaim "Tecole!" This was the call for the tecolero to apply the tar to the animal. It was not uncommon for it to also be applied to the nicks and small cuts that the shearers themselves might suffer during the day. Sometimes the word *tecole* could be confused by listeners as "coalie" since the shearers would yell out for tecole when needed. To one not knowing the term pronounced in Spanish, it sounded like "coalie."

The tecolero gradually disappeared from the shearing crews in the 1960s, as the blowflies were eradicated. Agricultural scientists developed a method to control the fly by sterilizing lab-raised blowflies in the pupa stage by exposing them to nuclear radiation. Those flies were then disseminated in great numbers that overwhelmed the native blowfly population. The small boxes of flies were dropped in the countryside from planes (Kelton 2007). The empty boxes that had contained the sterilized flies could be found on ranch pastures for many years.

Another method for application of the tecole to the injured animal was for the tasinque himself to apply it. The tasinques hated this method, for it slowed them down tremendously and meant a loss of money. It was not uncommon, in the days when tecoleros were still used, for a tasinque to ask the captain if it was his crew's requirement for the tasinque to apply the tecole; if so, the tasinque might avoid working on that crew. Thus, most captains employed tecoleros. Additionally, if the captain calculated how many fewer sheep a shearer would shear if also responsible for applying the tar, it made financial sense to employ a tecolero.

Shearers could often not avoid inflicting nicks and cuts on the animals. The animal always moved while it was being sheared, and the tools had to be extremely sharp so that the wool or hair could be cut. Indeed, every time the tools were sharpened, especially the combs, they developed extremely sharp-pointed ends. Those had to be filed down, or they would surely snag the animal's skin. Some men simply did not do a good job of filing down their tools. Others were known for their skill on how to file down (*dispuntar*) their combs. If this was done well, the comb would go through the wool/mohair very smoothly, would not snag in the fiber, and would not cut the animal. To make any money shearing, the shearer, who was always in a hurry, had to employ every little skill, such as being good at dispuntar.

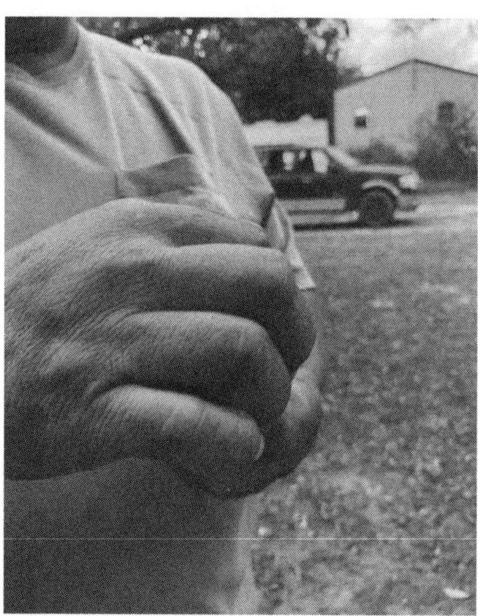

Isabel "Chavel" Sanchez, October 2020. *Dispuntar* was a necessary skill. Photograph from author's collection.

In locations in Texas where the sheep were sheared once a year, and in northern states such as Utah, Colorado, Montana, South Dakota, and Wyoming, it was necessary to employ an *amarador,* a man who would tie each fleece before it was packed. It was very important for a fleece to remain in one piece so that when packed, it would not blend into other fleeces and each fleece could be graded separately when unpacked at the mill.

The fleece was tied with a string made of a cardboard material. The fleece was rolled into a ball, the string tied once around the fleece and then crossed, and the string then tied in the opposite direction to form a perfectly tied round ball. The fleece was then taken to the empacadora to be packed. Sometimes the laneros were also the amaradores; however, large crews employed men to specifically do the tying.

The *corralero* was the shearing crew member who moved and secured the sheep or goats into the shearing pen. Sometimes the captain did this job, and often the laneros also participated, but the shearers never did since they were usually resting while the animals were penned. However, large crews often had a man whose only job was to pen the animals. It could be some older family member or shearer who could no longer shear but who was still given a job by the captain. It was not uncommon for captains to give positions to people who needed help but could no longer work as tasinques. These could be seen somewhat as charity positions, but it did provide the dignity of work and earnings to one who was still willing to work.

The corralero often had a docile lead sheep or goat (*sancho*) that would be trained to get in front of the animals to be penned. The animal would walk into the shearing pen, and the other animals would almost always follow. Many shearing crews had dogs that would travel with the crews, no matter where or how far they went, used to pen the animals to be sheared. Some dogs were legendary. Stories are told of dogs who were simply told, "go 'round," and they would get behind the animals and push them forward. Some were stubborn. For instance, Braulio "Bobby" Aguero, who was known for his well-trained Border Collies bred on the John Dooley Ranch, had a dog that the shearers said was supposed to be Queenie, but they called her "Dammit Queenie." The dog was so bad that Bobby would always yell, "Dammit, Queenie, go 'round." The corralero and his assistants, human or otherwise, were a critical part of the crew since animals were often difficult to pen and could delay a crew's work for long periods of time.

The *pora* on shearing crews was a sort of handyman. The word *pora* means "prep"; however, some people who know the shearing industry believe it came from the English word "porter," truncated and pronounced *pora* in Spanish. Some crews, especially the smaller ones, did not have a pora, in which case the captain would serve in the position. However, the position was one of helping the captain with a myriad of duties. It could be penning animals, sharpening tools, counting sheared animals as they left the pen, and doing other necessary jobs. The pora was ordinarily paid on a per-day basis. It was not uncommon for the pora to be the supervisor if the captain had to be absent from the crew. Usually held by persons who had been shearers at one time, this position was crucial for larger crews that could number from twenty to thirty shearers.

At times a crew did not have enough stations (drops) for all shearers. There might be twelve stations, but the captain did not want to leave out one more shearer to whom he had promised a job. In this case, a shearer was designated as the *extra*. This was usually one of the fastest shearers, and he would go from one station to another and shear three animals before moving on to another station. The shearer whose station the extra was using would take a short, welcome break, but some shearers resented losing out on shearing some animals and thus losing money. Or perhaps more important, they might get behind the shearer they were competing against. The extra would move his own headpiece from one station to another; he would not use the other shearer's tools.

One season, while shearing with the Frank Hidalgo crew, we went at night to shear the rams at another ranch while we were shearing on a different ranch during the day. The rams were so big that two of us had to shear one ram at a time. In my case, I would start it and shear halfway, and El Ruco would finish it. That night the late Leon Hidalgo and the late Aurelio "Welo" Fernandez, both big, strong men, were the extras. We looked forward to them getting to our stations. Paipe Aguero would implore Welo to hurry and get to his station quickly: "Vente angelon de la guardia, que ya me muero" (Come on, big guardian angel, 'cause I'm dying here!).

In describing shearing crews and its members, one is in essence listing a community of workers. It is more difficult to describe the many moments of exhaustion, monotony, loneliness, exhilaration, and tranquility experienced by such a community. However, all those members and moments made up the daily work of las máquinas.

6

The Tools of the Trade

MOST SPECIALIZED INDUSTRIES have tools that are unique to them; la trasquila was no different. For example, the engine that provided the power had its own interesting beginnings. First was the hand-cranked machine that powered the headpiece, which required at least two people to shear the animal. One would crank the machine, and the other would shear the sheep. Old shearers said that the cranker was as important as the shearer, since a steady, strong pace had to be maintained.

Hand-cranked shearing machine, Old Sonora Icehouse Museum, October 2020. Photograph from author's collection.

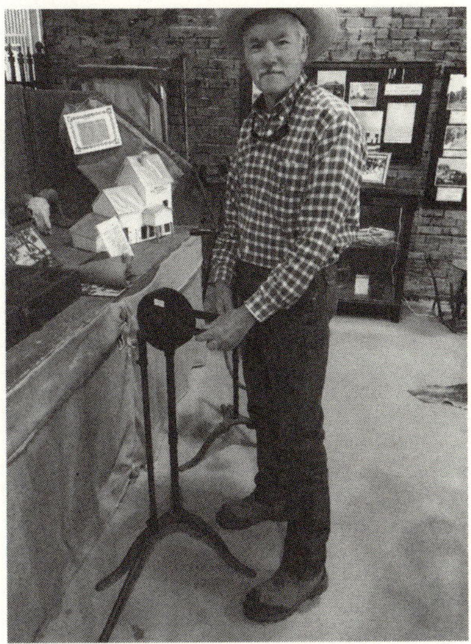

Edward Earwood of Sonora turning a crank-driven shearing machine, Old Sonora Icehouse Museum, October 2020. Photograph from author's collection.

Edward Earwood of Sonora indicated that his great-grandfather, Leven Edward Armer, was an engineer by trade and soon built a steam-driven shearing machine for his wife, Margaret, to help make the shearing easier. However, a picture of the steam-driven machine was not available. The next iteration of the shearing machine was a belt-driven system powered by a gasoline engine. Typically the engine (*ingenio*) was part of the truck, so it could be moved from ranch to ranch.

An *ingenio* near Belle Fourche, South Dakota, 1957. Photograph courtesy of Virginia Aguero Valenzuela.

A six-drop shearing machine at the Whitehead Museum, Del Rio, December 2019. Photograph from author's collection.

After some decades it became evident that the machine could be put on a trailer to remove the huge burden of purchasing, driving, and maintaining an old truck that could not be used for anything else. The trailer outfitted with the shearing machine could be easily moved about. However, it had its shortcomings too, since it put the loud, smoke-belching, hot motor right next to the shearers. These machines were prevalent in the 1940s through the late 1950s.

The advent of the electric motor changed the work dramatically. The motors were quieter, and the generator that powered the motors could be set outside the shearing pen, thus creating a much quieter, smoke- and heat-free shearing pen. The generator could also power fans for the shearers.

Shearers using electric motors on a ranch east of Sonora, 2020. Photograph from author's collection.

The instruments that actually cut the wool or mohair have also evolved over time. From the single knife blade that apparently was used in biblical times, to the scissor-type *tijeras trincas* that were utilized for decades, to the more recent headpiece (*mango*), all have served their purpose well. The current-day headpiece has not varied much over the years and continues to be the instrument of choice for shearers.

At the front end of the headpiece are the comb and cutter. The comb is attached first on the headpiece, and the cutter goes on top. As the fiber enters the teeth of the comb, the cutter moves back and forth over

Scissor-type clippers (*bottom right*), headpiece (*top*), and wool sack pins (*bottom left*), Davis Ranch, October 2020. Photograph from author's collection.

it and cuts the fiber. Combs came in iterations of seven, eight, nine, twelve, thirteen, and twenty teeth. The greater the number of teeth, the smoother the cut of the fiber. In other words, the more teeth on the comb, the less hair/fiber that would be left on the animal. The cutters had three or four blades. The comb and cutter are attached to the headpiece with a specialized screwdriver.

As the cutter moves over the comb, friction and heat develop. That friction is mitigated by applying motor oil to the cutter and comb when the headpiece is at a standstill. The oil was used at least once per animal

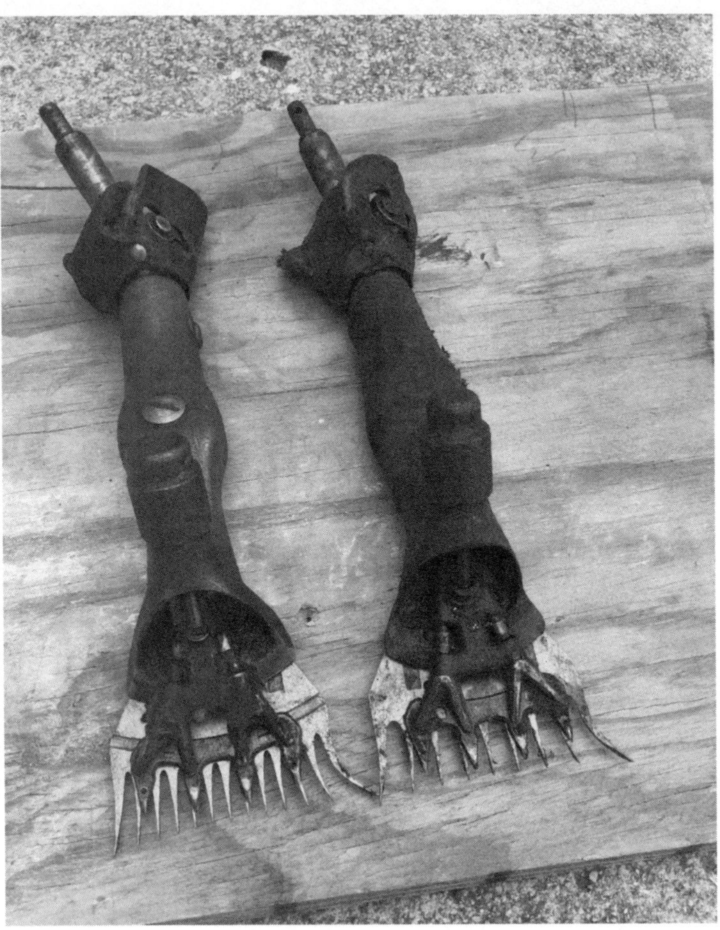

Two headpieces currently used by shearers. Photograph from author's collection.

Combs and cutters to be attached to the headpiece. Photograph from author's collection.

sheared. Any type of oil can will do, even old dishwasher bottles could be used as oil cans.

The cutter and comb were always kept razor-sharp, generally by the amolador, who initially sharpened the tools with a leather strap or a hand-sharpener stone. Eventually the tools were so numerous that they were sharpened with a rotating sharpener (*moyejón*). The first sharpeners were hand-cranked, then they were belt-driven, and currently they are rotated by an electric motor. A small square stone sharpener was also needed to blunt the very sharp points of the combs that developed as they were sharpened over and over again. The points were then smoothed over with sandpaper.

Once the shearer had cut the wool or mohair, it had to be packed for market. The lanero first carried it to a table where it was collected to be packed into a large burlap sack. The empacador proceeded to pack the fiber into the large sacks by getting in the sack and stomping the fiber down into the sack. The *empacadora*, a wood-framed contraption used to pack the fiber, has been reinvented over the years. From the wood frame to the metal frame to the cylinder-type to the new square packer, all have been used to pack, store, and eventually move the fiber to market.

Three-pronged screwdriver. Photograph from author's collection.

Hand-cranked tool sharpener. Photograph courtesy of Lee Sweeten.

Belt-driven sharpener. Photograph from author's collection.

Mohair collected at packing table. Photograph from author's collection.

Burlap sack used on the *empacadora* (formerly a wood-frame contraption, but metal in this case). Photograph from author's collection.

Rex Johnson sewing up a sack full of mohair, Rex Johnson Ranch, Rocksprings, 2018. Photograph from author's collection.

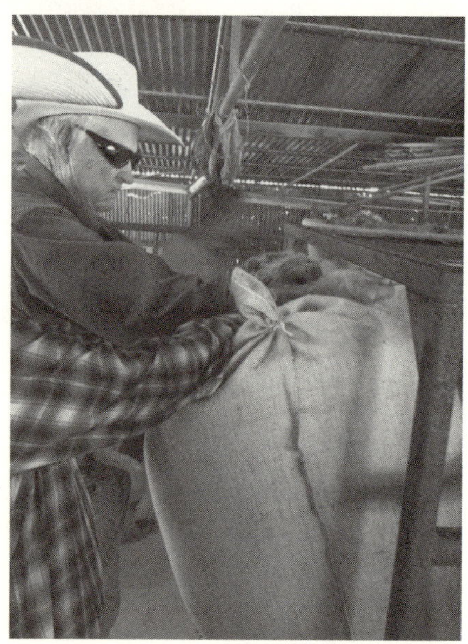

Cylinder packer from the Macario Aguero shearing crew. The *empacador* was Robby Garza. Photo taken in Utah, circa 1970. Photograph courtesy of Macario Aguero Jr.

Current-day square packer, Sonora Wool House Feed & Supply, 2020. Photo from author's collection.

Square sacks produced by the square packer, Sonora Wool House Feed & Supply, 2020. Photograph from author's collection.

7

Dancing with Sheep and Goats
The Techniques Used for Shearing in Texas

SOME DEPICTIONS OF HOW SHEEP were sheared in biblical times show that a knife blade was used to simply cut off the wool. Later in the development of the shearing technique, shearers began using scissor-type cutters. Shearing with the tijeras trincas was slow, and it was very difficult to run them smoothly and quickly over the animal's body. It also took a toll on the hands, wrists, and forearms of shearers as they constantly opened and closed the scissors to cut the fiber. In more recent times, shearers began to utilize the headpiece with the comb and cutter. Since then, the technique for shearing sheep and Angora goats the Texas way has not changed much. Over the centuries, the manner in which the animal was maneuvered, the strokes the shearer used, and the choreography utilized by the shearer have remained very much the same. Every stroke, every step, and almost every movement have been passed on from one generation of shearers to another by practice alone.

A typical day for the shearer begins with breakfast, though there were instances when some captains required shearing a pen full of goats before breakfast. After breakfast shearers would get their tools ready by making sure they had sharpened combs and cutters. They oiled their headpieces well and got ready for the first pen full known as *atajo* in Spanish. Generally the larger crews (six to twenty men) would have shearers on both sides of the machine. The sheep or goats would be driven into the shearing pen or arena on each side of the machine so that the men could select an animal to shear. The entire day was broken up by one pen full of goats or sheep after another.

To begin, the shearer had to select an animal from the atajo. Perhaps without realizing the importance of the skill of selecting the first animal, a newspaper article from the *San Angelo Standard-Times* described the men as beginning to work by selecting from the bunch one of "the easy-to-be-shorn": "When the *capitán* shouted *vamonos*, the men rushed forward and with great shrewdness selected an animal to shear. They selected small, light-wooled, the easy-to-be-shorn. As the loud sounds of the shears were heard it was not five minutes before a shearer was done shearing an animal" (Anonymous 1885). Various authors have also written of how shearers tentatively and carefully selected their first animal from a fresh atajo of sheep or goats: "[The shearer] felt critically of the wool on his sheep and then made [his] selection, caught the sheep dexterously by one hind leg, and dragged it, as it hops backwards, to the platform" (Kupper 1945, 153).

To an untrained observer the action of "felt critically of the wool" might seem a waste of time, since all the animals had to be sheared anyway. However, there were indeed logical reasons for being careful in selecting the first animal. The shearers understood that efficiency and speed were real factors influencing their work. Simply said, if they were to be paid per animal, speed and efficiency were tantamount to making more money. If one figured how many animals a shearer could shear over a season that could last as many as 150 days, any advantage became critical. Additionally, and perhaps more important, when shearers were competing to be the espada, any advantage paid off.

In selecting the first animal, the shearer generally wanted an animal that had less hair or wool, generally a *quatralva*, a sheep or goat that had little hair or wool on its stomach, feet, head, or underside of the neck. Selecting a quatralva would allow the shearer to quickly shear the animal, since shearing the feet was especially difficult and time-consuming. Some animals had lost their hair or wool because of shedding, and the shearers also quickly scooped up those. Jad Davis, an Angora goat rancher, said that he could typically cull his registered Angora goats by culling out the first ten or twelve that the shearers selected. Those goats were the ones that had produced less hair.

Second, the shearer generally selected smaller animals. The reasons were obvious: a small animal could be dragged to the station easily, could be sheared quickly since its low weight made it easier to handle, and had less surface to shear. Kid goats were often a pleasure to shear. Although loud, squirmy, and wild, they were not difficult to handle. Selecting a plump animal was also an advantage in that the headpiece could be run much more smoothly over the animal. A thin, bony animal presented problems, as it slowed down the shearer considerably. When one had plump quatralvas to select, they were a pleasure to shear.

Perhaps the foremost reason to carefully select an animal was the quality of its hair or wool. Ranchers and people who graded hair and wool by hand often said that if you watched which animals the shearers were shearing first, you would find those had the best-quality fiber. The shearer selected animals with good, clean, yet oily hair or wool. There was also a texture to some wool or mohair that was easier cut. The shearer made this careful selection so the cutter and comb attached to the headpiece would last longer before having to be changed out and sharpened. An animal with dirty, dry hair or wool would dull the shearers' cutters and combs so badly that they may have to change them before the atajo was done. This slowed down the shearer and of course wore down the tools more quickly. The tools were expensive, and the shearer bore that cost. Taking into account the length of shearing seasons, being careful on the selection of animals added up to more money being made and less cost for tool upkeep.

There were some exceptions in the consideration of these variables. For instance, sometimes rams or billy goats were mixed in with the atajo to be sheared. Those were generally bigger and had more hair or wool, but they were worth two tokens—twice the pay—so they were generally the first to be selected for shearing. Sometimes shearers were not particular with their selection; rather, they just grabbed the animal closest to them. Few if any shearers did this, but it did sometimes save time and energy to use that method.

Careful selection did not end with the first animal selected. It went on with every subsequent selection during the shearing of a whole pen. At every selection of an animal, speed, efficiency, and quality of the hair or wool were all considered, but it did not take much time to do so. After many years, shearers could quickly spot with one look the best and most choice animals available. Being able to do it well was a quality admired among shearers. As mentioned, the most-favored animals to shear were kid goats or lambs. Small and generally with fine hair or wool, they were quickly scooped up. It was somewhat exhilarating for the shearer to select kid goats or lambs that were quatralvas.

The most dreaded goats to shear were the mutton Angoras—those intended for eventual slaughter for their meat. They generally were big and heavy, had horns as big as those of the billy goats, and were usually much more agile, energetic, and wild than nannies, billy goats, or kids. And to the dismay of the shearer, they were worth only one token. They were also considered somewhat more dangerous to shear for fear of shearers cutting themselves since the mutton goats tended to move wildly through the shearer's stations. They were also notorious for running and jumping crazily when the shearer tried to capture them to drag to their stations. The jumping was especially scary, in that they could easily butt a shearer in the face as he bent over to grab the animal's hind leg. Often the shearer had to literally chase the goat down, and in that case the best place to grab it was by the hair under its chin. Again, shearers earned only one token for them, and they usually could count on shearing dramatically fewer during a work day due to the characteristics just described. For instance, a shearer might be able to shear 150 kid goats in one day but might be able to shear only 100 mutton goats in one day. Shearing at the Silver Lake Ranch, west of Camp Wood, was generally a nightmare because there were usually at least twenty thousand mutton goats on that ranch.

The favorite types of sheep to be sheared were those that had little wool or hair on their face, stomach, and feet, and the Suffolk breed of sheep was a prime example. The most dreaded were the Merino breed. The huge folds of skin under their necks were very difficult to shear, simply because one could not run the headpiece smoothly, thus slowing the shearer down considerably.

Once the animal was selected, it was always grabbed by the right hind leg. The sheep or goat had all its power in its hind legs, so the idea was to remove the right hind leg off the ground and make sure the left hind leg was slightly off the ground, thus removing most of the leverage the animal had to resist. The shearer had to be careful during this technique, since if the leg were pulled too high off the ground, it could be pulled out of the hip socket. However, if the leg was pulled correctly, the animal lost its power base and could be easily dragged to the shearing station. Seasoned shearers knew that the animal must be made to move quickly so that it could not resist. Although the heavier animals were more difficult to get to the shearing station, it could still be done efficiently. Efficiency and strength were very necessary, since the shearer would have to perform this lifting and dragging technique thousands of times during a season. Frankly, that was the most exhausting part of all the work to be done.

After having done the dragging technique thousands of times, the shearer developed an uncanny ability to know exactly when to turn the animal onto its left side and quickly position it at the shearing station. This was done by grabbing on to the wool or mohair on the animal's back and giving a quick yank downward. That skill took time to develop, but once mastered, it could be done without even giving it much thought:

> For the shearer, speed is the thing. The number of sheep a man can finish in a day determines his pay. If there is no lost time, this man can shear one hundred. Back at the platform, her fleece has been folded by the *lanero*, the boy who carries it to the big seven-foot bags that hang suspended from wooden frames. Meanwhile the shearer has mopped his brow and is ready for another sheep (Kupper 1945, 154).

Once the shearers had the animal at the shearing station, they had to quickly get it into position. However, there were two caveats that shearers had to follow. First, the overall idea was to have the animals stretched in such a way as to create a smooth shearing surface. The shearer held the headpiece in his right hand, but the left hand was constantly pulling the skin of the animal and was pushing the animal in such a way as to create a smooth surface. The smooth surface allowed the headpiece to flow smoothly and quickly and helped prevent the animal from being cut. If the animal was not stretched correctly, it seemed that the shearer was slowly poking and jabbing at the animal instead of smoothly stroking it. The feet and legs of the shearer also played a great part in maneuvering the animal. The feet were in constant motion and constantly pulling, pushing, holding, and stretching the animal. This is why the term "choreography" is often used in this book when describing the shearing techniques. Dancing with sheep and goats is an appropriate description.

Left-handed shearers had to learn how to shear with their right hand, because the drop was always positioned on the right side of the shearer, and if shearing left-handed, a tasinque would be facing the shearer next to him and thus creating a somewhat dangerous situation. Some shearers did use their left hand to shear, but seldom did it happen. Left-handed shearers who indeed learned how to shear with their right hand could be really good at it. The late Johnny Hernandez was such a case, and he was a docientero.

The headpiece was constantly rotating in the shearer's hand. The initial grip is similar to holding a tennis racket, but as the animal was moved and positioned in certain ways, the headpiece might have to be held upside down and moving downward or grabbed like a paint brush and moving upward. The constant rotating allowed the shearer to secure a better grip on the headpiece as shearing progressed and as the animal was moved around to create the smooth surface. This constant rotating was especially obvious as the shearer went up and down the legs of the animal and around its face, ears, or horns.

The first major move that a shearer conducted once at his station was to shear the belly (*pansiar*) of the animal. The animal was stretched so the headpiece could be run smoothly over the belly. Great care had to be exercised, since the animal was still untied and could kick the shearer or headpiece and possibly cause injury to itself or the shearer. In fact, this was the position in which shearers most often cut themselves. The strokes began at the area where the udders would be located on a female animal and moved toward the chest. When shearing sheep, the shearer had to remember to make the first stroke in front of the udder, from "west to east" (with the head as "north"). There was a large vein in the stomach in front of the udder that could easily be cut and produce a large flow of blood. If indeed cut, then the animal must be stitched up, or it could bleed to death.

In fact, shearers could often severely cut animals for a variety of reasons. The animal could move suddenly; the shearer may be going too fast and not being careful; or the combs could be too sharp at the points. After being sharpened many times, the tips of the ends of the combs would become like needle points that could easily penetrate the skin of the animal, and a severe cut could result.

If a severe cut was inflicted, the shearer would loudly exclaim, "Abuja!" This literally means "needle." It was a call for the captain to bring the needle and thread to stitch up the animal's cut. Some captains did not do this, and it was the shearers' duty to do their own stitching. Cuts in need of an abuja were never a good incident. The animal was cut, the shearer slowed down considerably, and the shearer could gain a reputation of being a bad cutter. Additionally, in the course of jugando pesado, there were always loud exclamations from other shearers as the

Jorge L. Gonzalez shearing the belly of an Angora goat at a ranch near Sonora, October 2020. Photograph from author's collection.

cry went out for an abuja. There could be many, but the jibe most often heard was, "Epale, el cocinero debe de matar los chivos, tu no" (Hey, the cook is supposed to kill the goats, not you). In reality, it was never very humorous, since cutting an animal seriously was often very upsetting to the rancher or owner. A crew could develop a reputation for being too careless. However bad the situation could be, cutting animals was never intentional, but in an industry where very sharp tools had to be utilized, cuts to the animals and the shearers were inevitable.

Once the belly was sheared, the shearer then sheared each leg, starting with the left hind leg. Great care had to be given here not to shear upward on the legs and perhaps cut the major tendon on the back of the leg. If this happened, the animal was incapacitated and probably would not survive at pasture. As the shearer moved from the left leg to the right, again great care had to be given, since here was where the shearer would shear the hair or wool off the female's udders. This had to be done so that the lamb or kid could suckle with greater ease. If cut, the teat on the udder would grow scar tissue over it, and the opening from which the lambs or kids got their milk would forever be closed, thus rendering that ewe or nanny almost useless for raising progeny.

The shearer's knees were constantly in motion during this phase of shearing, as they were placed on the floor and then moved onto the stomach of the animal to secure it in place. Care had to be given to not push too hard, or the animal would start to kick or squirm as it began to feel the weight on its stomach. This phase occurred thousands of times during the season and lifetime of the shearer. One can imagine the beating the knees took over the myriad times they were placed on hard wood or concrete floors.

Many videos of people shearing sheep generally show that the animal was not tied at any time during the process. This was a major difference between the technique used in Texas and the United States and the technique used in New Zealand and Australia. In those countries it was always the tradition to not tie the animals' feet while shearing them. In fact, when competing with shearers from around the world, Texan Gandy Hidalgo was penalized and lost points because he tied the animals and the other competitors did not. The judges felt that the animal was unduly roughly handled if one tied it. Gandy was as fast, sheared as cleanly, and handled the sheep as deftly as the other shearers, but he lost points and thus did not place in the top three for the international competition.

In the Texas way, the animal was always tied for a variety of reasons, but principally because that was the way shearers were taught, and those that came before them were taught the same way: in other words,

Angora goat being tied. Photograph from author's collection.

because of tradition. Presumably it began with shearers tying as many as ten animals at one time and shearing them with the scissor-type shears. Tying so many animals at one time cut down on getting up each time and having to go after another animal, and it allowed other hands to help the shearer bring the animals to the station. Tying so many animals at one time was later abandoned, as the size of shearing pens was reduced and as shearers lined up closer to one another; shearers simply did not have room to have ten animals tied in front of them at one time. Multiplied by twelve shearers, the situation just simply could not be accommodated.

Tying the animal occurred after the belly had been sheared. Generally shearers used a leather strap hitched under their belt as they went after another animal to shear. They used their hand to bring together the animal's feet, and once again the right knee came into play as it pushed the back legs of the animal forward so they could be intertwined with the front feet. Two loops were made around the feet: once around all four feet and then once around the front feet. The shearers were also taught a special knot to use to quickly tie the animal and not lose time. The knot was a form of slip knot that also could easily be untied when finished, thus allowing the shearer to quickly release the animal once it was completely sheared. I was taught the knot around a campfire by my brother Manuel and made to practice so I could utilize it right away. The knot, like much else about shearing, was handed down for many generations.

Once the animal was tied, a quick but very necessary action occurred. The shearer quickly grabbed the small oil can and oiled the comb and cutter on the headpiece. Good shearers oiled the cutter and comb only once per animal. Beginners would often have to stop and oil the tools midway through shearing an animal, since it took them a long time to shear it. Observers were always surprised at how hot the tools could be when they grasped the tools for the first time. But to a seasoned shearer, it was just another small irritant he had to endure.

The next major phase was to shear the neck, which the men called *pescuesiando*. It started with the shearer placing his left foot on the neck of the animal. It should be noted that the entire weight of the shearer's foot was never placed on the neck; rather, only the front of the foot was on the neck as the shearer's heel and full weight were on the floor. The shearer then pulled back on the tied feet with the back of his right leg.

When the foot was removed from the neck, the animal's head came up almost to the face of the shearer. The animal's snout was then held with the left hand and pushed back; thus the neck was stretched, which created a smooth surface to shear. If not stretched properly, the animal could be cut seriously.

The author shearing the neck of an Angora goat at a ranch near Rocksprings, May 2019. Photograph from author's collection.

Once the neck was sheared, the left hand was removed from the snout, and the head of the animal came back toward the shearer because the shearer's right leg pulled on the animal's tied feet. As the head of the animal came closer to the shearer, he was able to shear around the ears, horns, and eyes. Obviously, great care had to be taken here to not cut the animal's ear or eyes or the shearer's hands as the left hand came into close proximity to the headpiece while the ear was moved and sheared. Here the headpiece was used to push the ear forward so the shearer could go under and around it. Always aiming the headpiece downward so he did not cut the animal's eye, the shearer now sheared the forehead and snout. If the animal had horns, the headpiece must be handled deftly so it did not hit the horn and risk breaking an expensive comb or cutter. As careful as shearers were, sometimes cutting the ear, eye, or his own hand or breaking the tools did occur, always to the chagrin of the ranch owner, the captain, the shearer, or all three.

The next phase was referred to as the quartering phase (*cuarteando*). Not to be confused with butchering an animal into fourths, this phase was called "quartering" since the shearer was about a quarter-way done in shearing the animal. When teaching beginners, a seasoned shearer often quartered the animal and then handed it over to the beginner to finish. This was done so the beginner did not have to perform the two most meticulous and somewhat dangerous phases of shearing the belly (*pansiando*) and shearing the neck (*pescuesiando*). Over time the beginner learned to handle the headpiece and perform the strokes and was then allowed to shear an entire animal.

Quartering was done as the animal was on its back and as its left front leg was sheared in a downward fashion. The ribs were sheared at this time, and the shearer moved to shear the right side and back of the animal. One tactic taught to beginners and that seasoned shearers mastered was to shear as much of the rib area of the animal as far as they could reach while shearing the belly. Also in shearing the right leg, the shearer strokes as far toward the ribs and back as possible. This was done so that when the shearer was quartering the animal, the rib cage had already been sheared with quick, long strokes. If not done, the shearer lost time in shearing the ribs, because the animal was scrunched up since it was tied, and the shearer had to take time to try to poke at the hair/wool on the ribs: cumbersome, slow, frustrating work that could easily cut the animal, since the skin was bunched up. However, if done properly, the shoulder and ribs were sheared with three strokes, and the shearer moved on to the next phase, *a lo largo*.

Once the ribs had been sheared, the shearer moved on to the side of the stomach and the back of the animal. He used long strokes because he

The author quartering an Angora goat at a ranch near Rocksprings, May 2019. Photograph from author's collection.

began the strokes from almost the tail of the animal and moved toward the head. The shearer had been using rather short but somewhat smooth strokes on the belly, neck, and ribs, but now it was almost exhilarating to be able to use the long strokes. When the tools were sharp, the animal was plump, and the shearer had used his legs and feet correctly, only long, smooth, quick strokes come into play here. During this phase the shearer left the capasete on nanny goats. He simply left the mohair at a greater length instead of shearing it off completely from the back.

As the shearer finished the back of the animal, he moved on to the head. With goats, he did this by grabbing the left horn of the animal and shearing around the ears, eyes, and down the forehead. In shearing sheep, the shearer used his palm to hold the sheep's head as he moved to its head. The leg work came into close play here. To reach the head, the shearer used his right foot to position the animal. He moved the right foot over the back of the sheep and pushed back toward his body. This made the head of the animal come closer to him. He then took the snout of the sheep and turned it so the sheep was almost looking at him. This allowed him to move the headpiece around the right ear, down the neck, and toward the shoulder in a downward stroke. The shearer was now ready to finish the shearing.

The next phase, called sitting the animal (*sentando*), dramatically demonstrated the major difference between shearing sheep and goats. In shearing sheep, the shearer used his right foot to hook the tied feet of the animal and pick it up toward his face in order to sit the animal. There were some exceptionally strong shearers, such as Aurelio Fernandez and Leon Hidalgo, who did not use their feet to do so; they simply sat the animal using only their left arm to pull the animal up. However, most shearers did use their foot to sit the animal and began shearing the animal's right shoulder. Using long strokes, they then sheared in a downward fashion from the back of the animal toward the stomach. This allowed the shearer to quickly shear the ribs and legs of the animal all the way to the tail. At the tail the shearer used great care and a slower pace to be sure he did not cut the animal's anal area.

In shearing Angora goats, the shearer did not sit the animal; rather, he turned the animal upside down and sheared from the tail toward the head. This was termed *coliando*. After shearing the head of the goat, the shearer allowed the goat to fall to the floor and quickly grabbed its tail.

Using the tail, he quickly flipped the goat onto its head. He then sheared the animal's back and ribs, stroking from the stomach to the back. Once this was done, the shearer shut off the motor, set down the headpiece, untied the animal, grabbed it by its ear, stood it up, and pushed it toward the other animals in the pen. It was here when the shearer looked for his token.

The author shearing an Angora goat *a lo largo* using long strokes at a ranch near Rocksprings, May 2019. Photograph from author's collection.

Once the animal was released, the shearer quickly and deftly moved on to select another animal, and the process started all over again. As the animal was released, the lanero was waiting to hand the shearer his token, which was quickly put into a pocket. The lanero then scooped up the mohair or wool and took it to the table at the packing apparatus. In the 1980s many shearers began using clicker counters instead of tokens to keep a tally of the animals sheared in a day.

When a shearer released the animal, it went back to the others in the pen, which included the animals that had been sheared and those not yet done. As more animals that have been sheared joined the ones waiting to be done, it became more difficult to bring sheep back to the station or drop, because the shearer now had to fight through many animals to reach the unsheared ones mingled among the sheared. It was also very hard to pull an animal through a crowded pen. To alleviate this situation and when the electric motors came into popularity, shearers could now be strung out in a long row, thus eliminating the need to have shearers on both sides of the trailer. Shearers could then release backward (*soltar átras*). The shearers used the colloquial word *patras* instead of *átras*. As part of this method, a row of wool sacks was hung behind the shearers and their motors so that when the animal was sheared and released, it was pushed through the sack and into the pen behind the shearers. As more animals were sheared, only the unsheared ones remained in the forward pen. As the numbers dwindled, the shearer did not have to fight through the sheared animals to grab another animal. This was a minor development, but it increased the speed of the shearers and greatly reduced *el acarreo*, the burden of dragging animals to the drop. However, this was not practiced in many places in Texas, since the barns and pens were originally built to handle machines that accommodated shearers on both sides of it. This technique was never practiced while shearing Angora goats.

In summary, sleeping in a bedroll, getting up for breakfast, getting tools ready, and shearing all day were the norm for most men in shearing crews. It seemed monotonous; however, in observing seasoned shearers work, it was truly amazing how such actions as described in this chapter could occur in a matter of one to three minutes. In some ways, bull riding provides a good comparison. I used to assign a writing project to students in one of my college English classes, and a particular student-athlete on our rodeo team described what occurred in an eight-second bull ride. His meticulousness and attention to detail reminded me of shearing sheep and goats: so much happening in a short amount of time, and with one false move a lot of things could go wrong. Though shearing is not as dangerous as bull riding, the attention to detail that had to be paid in a short amount of time is comparable.

Shearing the head of an Angora goat. Photograph from author's collection.

But if all goes well, there are satisfaction and even exhilaration. When the tools were just right, the speed fast and smooth, and the animals plump and fine, there was almost exuberance as the shearer released the sheared animal. It was at those times that the songs came to the surface

Almost done. The Angora goat is now being sheared from the tail to the head. Photograph from author's collection.

and the friendly jeers at fellow shearers were shouted. "Como quiero a mi suegro José" (How I love my father-in-law José). And the response: "Mejor la pongo en los trackes" (I would rather place my daughter on the train tracks).

The author releasing the Angora goat on a ranch near Rocksprings, May 2019. Photograph from author's collection.

8

Los Tasinques
The Shearers

THE DAY FOR SHEARERS was quite simple. They rose early, had break-fast, and went to work. They sheared until noon, had lunch, and rested until about 1:00 p.m. They generally rested on the shearing floors, and discussions went on for the entire time. However, as the season wore on, it was very common to see the men napping for a short spell. Shearing then started again and went on until the herds were done for the day. This could be by 5:00 p.m. or as late as 7:00 p.m. They worked until all the animals for the day were sheared. Ranchers stressed that if the sheep or goats had lambs or kid goats and were not reunited with their mothers by the end of the day, then the mothers could abandon their young. This phe-nomenon was referred to as *se disaijan*, a colloquial expression meaning that the lambs or kids would not find their mothers at the end of the day.

Each day throughout the shearing seasons was by and large the same for the shearers. It was that daily repetition that made them experts at their trade, but it did not happen overnight. The "10,000-hour rule" promotes the idea that it takes about that number of hours to become an expert at a given task or subject (Gladwell 2008, 50). Although a precise calculation cannot be made of just when shearers become experts, most would agree that it would take about three years.

In the shearing pens, it was sometimes said, "En cada cabeza un mundo" (In each head another world), which applied to each shearer who ever sheared sheep or goats. Shearers came in all sizes and shapes, from the hulking Arturo Sanchez of Sonora to the muscular Leon Hi-dalgo and the slight but lithe Manuel Aguero Jr., both of Camp Wood.

Shearers at a ranch near Sonora, 1949. Russell Lee Photograph Collection, e_rl_14233_0017, The Dolph Briscoe Center for American History, The University of Texas at Austin

They included men such as Israel Falcon, who literally died while shearing sheep. Another was Leonard "Boy" Hernandez, who sheared until the large herds of animals ceased to exist and then went on to form a successful fence-building company. There were thousands of shearers throughout the era of la trasquila, and they came from all over Texas, California, Colorado, Mexico, and other places. They were part of crews that numbered as little as two men or as many as thirty-two. All the men and women who made up the crews—the captain, the lanero, the cocinero, and others—were very important, but without the shearers, the work of shearing did not exist.

It is impossible to tell the story of each and every one of them, so I have provided the stories of some I have spoken to and who have great and vivid memories of their work as shearers. In the personal interviews one can see that many of them indeed had lives of hard work but also of great joy, a strong belief in religion, and intense love for their families.

It is important to record their memories of sheep and goat shearing, since the existing pictures too often depict them only as sweating men bent over with their heads down. Thus, it becomes important to give life to those pictures. Accordingly, provided herein are interviews and life vignettes of los tasinques, the men who did the work of shearing sheep and Angora goats.

Many authors refer to them in broad strokes: "There were Mexican men." Others said that "the Mexicans came on horses" or that "the shearers were Mexicans." But sadly for their descendants, their names were seldom provided in the literature, and their names will be lost to history as the shearing industry fades. Therefore, this chapter seeks to give life, names, and identity to men who did the work of shearing so that some record can be kept of their traditions and work. Although shearers were almost mechanical in their work, they were not machines; rather, they all had lives, families, and stories to tell. Here are three of them.

Gaudencio "Gandy" De Leon Hidalgo

Guadencio is better known as Gande, or Gandy, which was the name his mother gave him when he was a child. He was born to Manuel Salazar Hidalgo and Maria Nevarez De Leon in Camp Wood on February 12, 1931. His father, who was born in 1903, came to the Montell and Camp Wood area in 1921 at the age of eighteen along with his friend Teodoro Valenzuela, both from Musquiz, Mexico. They came to cut cedar in the Camp Wood area. Manuel and Maria courted in the Montell area, where Maria resided. They were soon married and eventually had twelve children. All five boys, Leon, Sadot, Enrique, Frank, and Gandy, would eventually become shearers in their father's crew. After Manuel grew older, Frank and Gandy took on the role of captains and ran the crew in Texas and South Dakota, Wyoming ("Guayoma," as Gandy said it), and Montana.

Gandy met Lucinda Perez in the early 1950s in O'Donnell, as both were doing migrant work in the cotton fields of the area. She was originally from Musquiz but now made her home in Rio Grande City along the Mexico-Texas border. She and her family had come to the United States on a work permit and just stayed. A romance was soon under way, and they were married in O'Donnell in the former schoolhouse where

Gandy and Lucinda Hidalgo. Photograph courtesy of Greg Hidalgo.

their families lived during the migrant work season. Gandy remembers that they slept on the floor. Later Lucinda helped Gandy's mom cook for the Frank Hidalgo crew. She was also a lanero for some time before they had children. Gandy and Lucinda were married for sixty-three years. They had nine children: five boys and four girls. Tony and Jesse became shearers, and Steven did too for a short time. One of Tony's boys, Tony Jr., also learned how to shear; however, he was the last of Gandy's lineage to do the work.

In his youth Gandy was five feet, nine inches tall and weighed from 160 to 180 pounds. At the age of eighty-eight, Gandy was still tall, and he has a clear mind and vivid memory. His demeanor is somewhat similar to that of Hollywood's Gary Cooper: he is quiet and speaks slowly. He recalled that his father taught him how to read and write before he went to school, but he was taught in Spanish. He was moved up to the third grade very soon, but when he was nine years old, he asked his father if he could quit school and join his sheep-shearing crew. His dad agreed, so at the age of nine Gandy became a lanero. After about three years he was moved up to empacador, where he spent another three years tromping and packing wool and mohair. Then at the age of fifteen he became an *aprendiz* (apprentice) shearer. He held all of these positions with his father's shearing crew. There was no looking back after that; he was in it for the long run. He was very good at shearing and was often the espada on the crews. The most sheep he sheared in one day was 203, and the most goats was 233—truly amazing.

He remembers well his days spent on the shearing crews. He sheared with Frank, his brother, and the Feliz Carabajal crew of Belle Fourche, South Dakota. However, his first trip north was with a crew from Uvalde. He remembers that they spent a whole week on the road to get to South Dakota, and the return trip also took a week. The trucks were old with no cover for the back, so they simply rode on top of all the bedrolls that were thrown in the back. Their food on the road was, as Gandy describes it, *lonche frio* (cold lunch). They stopped for breaks along the road but seldom in restaurants or other places of business. At that time, Gandy recalls, they were not allowed to enter those places because they were "Mexicans." He remembers that racism was always around in those days.

Gandy remembers very well that once they arrived at the ranches, they sheared continually until the season was over. They slept on the ground in bedrolls that consisted of a small mattress, quilts, blankets, and a tarp to cover themselves if it rained. The captain or rancher never provided bathing and toilet facilities. The crew simply cleaned up from water troughs or water tanks.

Gandy also remembers that the food was always good but never seemed to vary. Typically they had whatever *carne* (meat) the rancher provided, and at times this included antelope meat. However, it was usually lamb or, in Texas, goat (*cabrito*) most of the time. Beans were a staple, as were tortillas. Breakfast was eggs, coffee, tortillas, and the ever-present beans. However, the captains did provide a 10:00 a.m. break for coffee and a quick bite. In those days they sheared an atajo before breakfast, so they needed the morning break for sure. Since they generally worked late, a 4:00 p.m. break, sometimes referred to as the merienda, was provided. You simply had to work until all the sheep for that day were sheared. It if was a big herd, you kept going, so the merienda was very necessary. This break also featured coffee with some snack such as tortillas with molasses. Gandy remembers that once on his brother Frank's crew, Lucia, Frank's wife, was the cook, and she prepared *empanadas* (turnovers) for the merienda; however, she sold them to the tasinques for a check (a token for one sheep sheared). It did not matter; they thought it was a great deal. Gandy's dad was often the cook, but his mother, Maria, and his wife, Lucinda, also cooked for the Manuel Hidalgo crew at one time or another. They camped at the ranch and cooked on the ground over an open fire.

Being a superior shearer, Gandy made money. He remembers that his father bought him a brand new 1956 Chevy sedan because Gandy and his father had a unique business arrangement: when Gandy worked on his father's shearing crew, they did not keep records of how many sheep Gandy sheared during the season. His father simply gave him money when he needed it.

Later in life Gandy seized on a business opportunity in Camp Wood and bought a Texaco gas station. He left the shearing business for eighteen years while he and his sons ran the gas station. Gandy said he took on the station because his wife did not want him to be gone for long periods of time, such as when they went north to shear. They now had kids in school who needed him. Lucinda wanted him to find something in Camp Wood, so when the Texaco opportunity came up, he took it. A fuel dealer from Rocksprings brought him loads of gas and oil to sell, but most important, Gandy's dad helped him with money to get the station started. Again, Gandy and his dad kept no books.

One day a man from the Nevarez family asked him to compete in shearing competitions. Gandy competed in San Angelo in 1982 and 1983. He won first place in both of those years and was declared the Texas State Champion. In 1991, he was again state champion and was then invited to the international competition in Denver, Colorado. He competed against shearers from all over the world. He won ninth place out of forty shearers and just missed the finals. He lost points because he tied the animal, the technique Texas shearers use. The judges deducted points from Gandy because they considered tying the animal as too rough, and the handling of the animal was a criterion in judging the competition. He won a ribbon at that competition, and Gandy said he was more proud of that ribbon than of all his championship buckles. "For you see," he said, "I competed against the best in the world."

When asked about special memories regarding his shearing days, Gandy recalled shearing 233 Angora goats in one day. It was in the 1980s, and he was shearing with the Manuel "Gugo" Aguero Jr. crew. They were in the Loma Alta area, and Cayetano, Roberto, Kinilio, and Joe Falcon were with them that day. Joe and Kinilio also sheared over 200 that day, but Gandy was the espada.

When asked what other great shearers he remembered, Gandy recalled Ben "El Chueco" from Uvalde. The man limped badly, but he was a great shearer. Gandy was a lanero on the crew that year, but he remembers he wanted to be just like El Chueco when he became a shearer. Manuel "Gugo" Aguero from Camp Wood also immediately came to his mind. However, he also remembered Juan Falcon, who was the father of the Falcon men just mentioned. He recalled Javier De Leon, and Don Lupe De Leon and his boys, Cruz, Liborio, Felix, Rey, Lupe Jr., and Teddy. He remembered *los Nevarez*: Toribio, Amado, and Don Polo Nevarez. He recalled Gabino Fernandez and his son, Aurelio. He of course remembered all of his brothers and one special occasion when Gandy, his brother Leon, and their cousin Chavel Ortiz competed during a hot day in August as they were shearing Angora goats. All three were great shearers, but Gandy beat them both that day. He recalls that his father told them, "Gandy is older and married, but he still can beat you two."

Gandy recalled that in 1949 his dad's crew sheared around Pumpville ("Pompil," as Gandy says it), where the crew sheared about thirty thousand Angora goats. There were six shearers on his crew at the time. His father had a wreck on their way to shear at a ranch near Del Rio. They went off a bridge, but no one was seriously hurt (although Polo Saiz hurt his leg).

When asked what would he have done if he had chosen a different career, his response was not surprising: "I grew up shearing and working the fields . . . cotton, potatoes in Colorado, so I never thought of another career. I made good money. It was a good career and I would not change it."

Another question: "What do you want people to remember about la trasquila?" He replied, "In those days it was something we were proud to do, since we could provide for our families." He continued, "I do not remember not having work . . . the field work, shearing. . . . We always had work."

Gandy told me that he stopped shearing in 2010 to take care of his wife, who was ill with a terminal disease. Gandy had also lost three daughters to cancer, and his wife later succumbed to her disease. Gandy's strong belief in God and the Catholic Church helped him remain strong. He said that his belief started early at the age of fifteen when he would organize church festivals, prayer groups, *via cruzes* (way of the cross), *rosarios* (rosaries), Virgen de Guadalupe processions, and *posadas.* The posadas are the reenactments of Mary and Joseph seeking lodging in Bethlehem. In those early days the priest would come once a month from San Antonio or Uvalde to celebrate Mass in Camp Wood. As a result there were few church services, so Gandy took it upon himself to bring people together for church events. On one occasion a priest from Uvalde was serving the Camp Wood community, but he could not read in Spanish. He asked Gandy to do the readings in Spanish, and from then on Gandy was a church leader.

Gandy also served as an educational leader, as he was the first Hispanic person from Camp Wood to serve on the Nueces Canyon Consolidated Independent School District (ISD) board of trustees. However, perhaps the most long-lasting gift to the Camp Wood community was that Gandy, along with other Hispanic men of Camp Wood, helped literally build the Catholic Church on the west side of Camp Wood, where West Side Park is currently located. In addition, in the early 1970s, Gandy again helped construct what is now St. Mary Magdalen Church in Camp Wood. He and Antonio Vandivia constructed the church.

It can be said with true conviction that the men of Camp Wood respected Gandy because of his great skills in shearing sheep and goats. He was highly respected by the community at large for his work with the public schools as he served on the Nueces Canyon ISD school board. Most important, Gaudencio Hidalgo was respected by the community and the Catholic diocese for his work with the Catholic Church in Camp Wood. In recognition of his work, he received one of the highest awards a lay person could receive from the Catholic Church, presented to Gandy by the bishop of the San Antonio Diocese. These were proud moments for Gandy, his family, and the community of Camp Wood.

Sadly, Gandy Hidalgo died tragically in a car accident about two months after our interview. Hundreds of people attended his funeral. He is interred in the Camp Wood cemetery.

Manuel Aguero Jr.

When shaking hands with Manuel Aguero Jr., one was immediately impressed by two things. First, it felt as if you were shaking hands with an oak tree branch; his hands were very callused and rough. Second, you noticed the strength in his hands. There was a hand-wrestling game that was often played in the barrios whereby you interlocked middle fingers with an opponent and then tried to turn the other person's wrist. Manuel was the unofficial champion in Camp Wood. He resided in Camp Wood with his wife of over fifty-five years, Mary De Leon Aguero. They had six daughters and many grandchildren.

The calluses and roughness of Manuel's hands are due to the more than sixty years of cutting cedar, building fences, and shearing sheep and Angora goats. He is best known in shearing circles as "El Gugo," a nickname his brother gave him as a boy. It has no real meaning, but if you ask shearers about Gugo, they generally shake their heads and say that he was *la mera sorga* (best of the best).

Our entire interview was conducted in Spanish. He was the son of Manuel Aguero Sr. and Francisca Martinez Aguero. Gugo said that his father came from Sabinas, Coahuila, Mexico, in 1910. Manuel Sr. had

Manuel Aguero Jr. shearing the rams on the Carson Ranch, circa 1985. Photograph from author's collection.

to look for work when he suddenly became the head of the family when his father was killed in a mining accident in El Tiro de San Felipe mine. A gas explosion in the mine killed many men and left Manuel to become the provider for the family of two brothers and two sisters. He found work on the Tom Beck Ranch west of Barksdale and settled into vaquero work.

Manuel Sr. met Francisca Martinez, one of the three Martinez girls of Barksdale. The other sisters were Gregoria and Emeteria, daughters of Macario and Concepcion Martinez. Concepcion became a widow and was known as "Old Marie" in the Anglo community in Barksdale. She sold tamales, made beer, put on patio dances, was a midwife, and prepared bodies for burial to make ends meet for her family of four, including one son, Victoriano. According to Concepcion, she was a full-blooded Apache.

In 1915 Manuel Sr. married Francisca in Barksdale, and they settled on the Mamie Powers Ranch west of Barksdale. They had eleven children of whom Gugo was the second youngest. He was born on the Powers Ranch on January 15, 1938. Gugo said that he was delivered by the rancher's wife.

The rancher, Kirk Kirchner, allowed Manuel Sr. to run some goats and sheep on his ranch as part of his pay and to make ends meet for his large family. The boys grew up as cowboys too; however, to save money, Manuel Sr. sheared the goats himself. As the boys got older, he taught them how to shear his goats along with the rancher's goats and sheep. When the rancher retired, Manuel had to move his family to Camp Wood, then a thriving small town. Two of the boys, Leandro and Octaviano, "Tano," started their own shearing crew. Eventually, brothers Braulio, Macario, Hilario, and Gugo sheared on the crew. Other members were their great-uncle Braulio and brothers-in-law Keno Falcon and Marcos Ortiz Sr., as well as Castulo Saiz and Chicho Vara, also from Camp Wood.

Gugo dropped out of school after the fourth grade to become a lanero, an empacador, and by the age of thirteen, a tasinque. He learned to shear by watching and by jumping off the empacadora to shear a goat when the shearer might be taking a break. The older brothers knew Gugo was going to be special when on his first day of shearing full-time, he sheared more than one hundred Angora goats. He went on to become an exceptional shearer who sheared as many as 315 goats in one day. The most sheep he sheared occurred in South Dakota, some 286 in one day; both were incredible numbers.

On the day of our interview, Gugo showed no evidence of gaining weight with the years. He was a lithe five feet, seven inches tall and weighed about 150 pounds. He was eighty-one years old and had a clear and vivid memory. Not big for a superior shearer, he nevertheless always had great strength in his hands and substantial endurance. An incredible competitor, he always wanted to be the best, even at picking cotton. On the shearing crews, he was always the espada. He would compete the entire five-month-long season to keep his position and did so for over forty years.

During his career Gugo started going to South Dakota, as he and Joe Falcon of Camp Wood were laneros for the Felix Carabajal crew of Belle Fourche. Later he sheared with his brothers' crew in South Dakota and Texas. He also sheared on the crew of his brother-in-law, Rey De Leon, in the Dakotas. He spent many years shearing with the Nino Garduña crew of Belle Fourche. That crew traveled the state of Montana from Jordan to Glasgow and also went to Cutbank. Often they would also shear in North Dakota and Wyoming. He traveled to Montana to shear with the Lico Reyes crew of Uvalde; there too, he was the espada. He said he enjoyed working with Nino Garduña because he was a good man and his boys, Nino Jr. and Alfred, were good people. Don Nino was willing to work hard and pay as well as other captains, Gugo said. "He would work you as hard as you wanted to." Gugo recalls that once he needed five more sheep sheared to reach two hundred, and he asked Don Nino to put them in. He did!

For much of his shearing career, Gugo also sheared on his brother Tano's crew. Their work was almost entirely in and around the spot-in-the-road town of Loma Alta, which is between Sonora and Del Rio. He remembered the ranchers as the Whiteheads: Bill, Sonny, Willie B., and Lee. He remembered the crew of ten men spending an entire month on the Whitehead ranches before they had sheared all of their Angora goats. Those were not all the goats they sheared, since he remembered other ranches known to the shearers as *el rancho de los blanquillos* (ranch of the eggs), *rancho de los Galloways, el Finegan, el Lloyd, rancho del gorrudo* (man with the big hat), and *el rancho del paralis* (a rancher who was paralyzed.)

A special memory he has is of the Silver Lake Ranch, which lies west of Camp Wood and is accessed by the Tularosa Road, off Farm to Market Road 334, between Laguna and Brackettville. The ranch consisted of thousands of acres; it was so large that it had various sub-ranches within it. The sub-ranches were the Norias Dobles (double wells/windmills), Lost Creek, White Valley, and the headquarters ranch. One of the pastures was known as Los Alemanes (the Germans) because of its proximity to a massacre that occurred at the site on the Nueces River during the Civil War. Gugo's memories are astounding.

Manuel recalls shearing over twenty thousand mutton goats on the sub-ranches of Silver Lake. As mentioned, the goats were very large, had long horns, and were wild, since they were rounded up only twice a year for shearing. It was a circus when they were driven into the shearing pen. He forlornly remembers waking up to find three thousand goats coming down a hill with their huge horns shining in the morning sun and knowing he had to shear all of them.

When asked what they ate at work when de campo, the answer was not surprising: meat provided by the rancher, beans, tortillas, potatoes, and coffee. One of the cooks was his mother, known as "Wela Kika." A special treat that she prepared was the bread called pan de campo. At another time that he sheared with his brother Tano's crew, the cook was Lala Aguero, Tano's wife. She cooked out of the chuck wagon–type school bus. The cook on Lico Reyes's crew in Montana during the summer of 1966 was a man called "La Becerra" (the heifer).

He remembered taking a quick break for coffee in the morning because the crews started shearing at 6:00 a.m. He commented that the captains "te tenian impuesto a que todo tenia que ser pronto" (the captains had us used to the idea that everything had to be done quickly, even the break). The usual merienda at about 4:00 p.m. was necessary because they often had to work late. He recollected lovingly that his sister-in-law Lala would bring them *pan dulce* (Mexican sweet bread) from Del Rio at times for the merienda. She was very special to him.

A memory still vivid in Gugo's mind was the time a skunk bit him at el rancho de los blanquillos near Loma Alta. He had rolled out his bed on the barn floor one night, and the skunk came out from under the barn floor as they were all sleeping. He felt something at the top of his head. As he awoke in pain, he grabbed the skunk by the throat and pulled it from his head, removing some of his own hair in the process, and he choked the skunk to death. He woke up his brother Tano and sister-in-law Lala, and they drove him to the hospital in Del Rio. They had taken the dead skunk with them, and it was sent off for testing for rabies since the doctor thought that if a skunk had attacked someone at night, there was something seriously wrong with the skunk. Tia Lala heard the comments about the rabies and was somewhat frightened as she tended to be *bien miedosa* (easily scared) anyway, as Gugo remembered it. He remembered driving back to the ranch and Lala sitting extra close to her husband in the cab of the pickup and away from Gugo. He said he didn't do it, but just for fun he wanted to growl and snap at Lala. He laughed heartily at this memory. But sure enough, the skunk tested positive for rabies and Gugo had to have seventeen shots in his abdomen for preventing rabies. He didn't like the shots, but he hated more so having to stay at home and not being able to shear during the heart of the season.

A story that is almost mythical in shearing circles is the story of Gugo being a heavy coffee drinker. Gugo recalled that they were camped out at a ranch in West Texas and it had rained for about three days in a row. The men passed the time in an old house playing a card game called *malia*, which can go on for hours at a time. Paipe Aguero was watching, tending the coffee pot, and Gugo kept asking him for a cup of coffee. When Paipe saw that the cups were going to be many, he started counting them. Gugo drank twelve cups of coffee while playing cards. As they were about to break up the game and go to bed, Paipe asked Gugo if he wanted one more cupful, since it was the last one in the coffee pot. Gugo responded, "No, me puede hacer mal" (No, it could make me sick).

Other memories of la trasquila for Gugo are the ranches: some beautiful, but some with pens and corrals and nothing else. He remembered shearing two hundred or more sheep every day at thirty cents per head and said that sixty dollars per day in those days was quite a bit of money. His memory wandered back to sleeping in barns during the winter in the Dakotas and Montana and of making small tents over his bed with the tarp used to roll up his own bed to keep out the snow and cold. Gugo spoke of the accommodations as usually being ranch barns, sheep-shearing sheds, or the open sky. He slept in his bedroll on the floor or perhaps on army cots made of canvas. Restroom and showering facilities were not available; he simply did not bathe. Gugo eventually would run his own crew of seven or eight men who sheared Angora goats in Texas. They would shear twenty thousand Angora goats for the Perry Bushong Ranch as well as thousands more for other ranchers, including the Charles Carson ranches.

He also said that he eventually bought a building in downtown Camp Wood and started a restaurant called Manuel's Tacos. Mary and their daughters did the cooking and the waiting on tables; Gugo washed dishes. They did very well with the business, and their food was good. However, he remembered that the dishes sometimes went unwashed as he would often go out to the tables and sit with patrons, drink coffee, and strike up conversations.

When asked who were other tasinques he sheared with and that he remembered, his first response was that there were just too many to remember all of them, but offhand he recalled his brothers and named each one: Lel, Leandro, Maque, Bobby, and Layo. He remembered his brother-in-law, Marcos Ortiz Sr., and Marcos "Pico" Ortiz Jr. He also recalled Chal Galvan, Chendo Saiz, Ruben Balderas, Jimmy Balderas Jr., Chema Uvalles, Welo Hernandez, and Gabino Fernandez. He had a special memory of Gabino Fernandez, who was a small, dark-complexioned man who loved to laugh. In their youth Gabino and Chente Sena would compete against each other every day for the entire season. He said, "Se agaraban bien a bien" (They would get after it). He remembers others such as Paipe and Borao Aguero, Boy and Juan Hernandez, Beto Falcon, Keno, and Gome Falcon, as being exceptional shearers.

In retirement, Gugo could often be found on his front porch, waving to friends and neighbors as they drove down his street. Few vehicles passed without a honk or a wave; Gugo was very well-known. Even the school kids knew him and listened to his comments as they went by.

He often also held court with his stories of years gone by. He will tell you sincerely that he worked until his body could not do it anymore. He is slightly stooped, as are many old shearers, but still vigorous in his older age. In fact, it is almost a miracle that Gugo was still alive. A few years back he suffered a debilitating stroke and was in the hospital. The doctors called the entire family together and informed them that he would not survive the night. The next prognosis was that if he survived, he would be relegated to a vegetative state. The next prognosis was that he would need much physical therapy, since he could not talk and had no memory.

He received the speech and physical therapy and healed completely. He had great doctors, but because of his family's strong belief in God and their continual prayers for him, he believed in the miracle.

My final question to him was what I should say about la trasquila for future generations who would read his interview. His sincere answer was that he did it for his family. He said, "I wanted my girls to have schooling; I did not want them to work like I did. I wanted the best for them." Gugo went on to say that it was hard but honest work. "With shearing I raised my girls quite comfortably. I cut cedar; I made fences for twenty-five dollars a day for Old Man Charles Carson. I made an okay living. I have nothing to complain about."

A very affable man, Gugo would engage anyone in conversation and would always have a great shearing story to tell. Sadly, Manuel Aguero Jr. passed away in May 2021. He was so looking forward to the publication of this book. He is interred at the Camp Wood cemetery.

Felipe Valverde Martinez

Felipe Valverde Martinez, 2019. Photograph from author's collection.

When I met Felipe, I couldn't believe he was ninety-six years old. He is brown complexioned and had a wrinkled face; however, his dark brown eyes were just as clear as his speech and his memory. Amazingly, he still walked around with no assistance when we met at the front gate of his home in Brackettville. Felipe had the leathery look and complexion of men who have worked outdoors all of their lives. As we began the interview, he told me that he would not mince his words: "sin pelos en la lengua" (with no hairs on the tongue).

Felipe was born on November 27, 1922, and resided at his birthplace, Brackettville, for most of his adult life. Brackettville is in Kinney County in Southwest Texas, about forty miles from the Mexican border. However, he and his siblings were raised in Montell. As he reminisced, hand on his forehead and slightly bent at the table, Felipe remembered that his father, Felipe Sr., came from San Buenaventura, Mexico. His grandfather was Victoriano Martinez, also from Mexico.

According to Felipe Jr., and like many men at the time, Felipe Sr. came looking for work. He and his brothers Macario and Francisco crossed at the US-Mexico border at Piedras Negras, which is situated right across the border from Eagle Pass. Felipe Sr. often told his family that they each paid five cents at the international bridge when they crossed at Piedras Negras, with no questions asked. Macario went on to Barksdale, or La Villa, as the Hispanic families called it in those days. According to Felipe Jr., Macario married Conception Lopez, who later, as a widow, was known as "Old Marie" in Barksdale. Her daughters were Emeteria, Francisca, and Gregoria, and her son was Victoriano. The daughters eventually had large families who resided in the Edwards Plateau and the Nueces Canyon area. Emeteria married Rafeal Garduña, Francisca married Manuel Aguero, and Gregoria married someone whose name Felipe could not remember, "but he was from Rocksprings," he said.

Felipe Sr. found work cutting cedar, building fences, clearing land, and working on ranches as a vaquero in the Montell area of the Nueces Canyon. He met Isabel Valverde, daughter of Juanita Valverde, of Montell and they soon married. They had ten children, including Felipe Jr. He recalled that his mother, *la viejita* (the old woman) as he called her, would often run them all off from the house in Montell, including his father. They would go to Brackettville and reside for a while, but soon the old couple would get together again. He laughingly said, "No se querian" (They did not like each other). I sat across the table from Felipe in the house he and his wife, Saida, built. He said, "The lot belonged to my in-laws, but they sold it to us."

Felipe's schooling was not lengthy. He recalled going as far as the third or the fourth grade in Brackettville. He quickly added, "But I am not ignorant!" Although our interview was conducted in Spanish, he told me in very clear English that he could read and write in Spanish and English and had always made his own calculations during his work life. He said, "I taught myself, and I can show you if you want!" He proudly read the Bible every day and said, "Le pido a Dios que me deje llegar a cien años" (And I ask the Lord to let me live to be a hundred).

During his trips to and from Montell, Felipe met the young Saida Uvalles, and they courted. As was the formal custom of the times, his father and mother wrote a letter to Saida's parents to seek permission for Felipe to visit their home and ask for her hand. Indeed, they were granted the permission, and he went to the house of his future bride. At that meeting he was granted their blessing to marry Saida. They were married on August 27, 1944, at the old Catholic church in Brackettville, and the marriage lasted for seventy years, until Saida's death at the age of ninety. They had fourteen children: six boys and eight girls. Felipe proudly remembers all of their names and where they now reside. His eyes tear up as he remembers Ambrosio, who was his oldest son and who died at a very young age. He quietly and bitterly says, "por la desgraciada tomada" (because of the damn drinking). He does not remember the names of all his grand- and great-grandchildren, but he laughingly says, "I used to keep the names in a little notebook, but there were so many I had to throw the book away."

Felipe says that when work would dry up in the Montell area, they would go back to Brackettville to work the ranch his father owned. It was a section of land, 640 acres, located between Brackettville and Laguna on Farm to Market Road 334. They ran Angora goats and sheep in the section, and his uncle Francisco Martinez sheared their goats and sheep. Thus, Felipe was introduced to shearing. However, their small ranch and animals could not sustain the entire family, so Felipe went to work on his uncle Francisco Martinez's shearing crew, which consisted of eight shearers.

As did most young men on shearing crews at the time, he started out as a lanero. Soon the older shearers taught him how to shear. First they would quarter (*quarteaban*) for him, but at the age of fourteen he became a full-fledged shearer, earning four cents per head. Felipe remembered that by that time in 1936, shearers were already using the belt-driven clutches, drops, and headpieces.

He remembered that later, as a grown man, he went to California to shear sheep with Captain Reymundo Talamantes of Brackettville. They did not shear many, since the herds were small, but his greatest memory is the captain flying him to California. Although most of the men took small campers on the back of trucks or drove their own cars, he was flown! He earned nineteen cents per head at the time. He said they ate potatoes and beans and sometimes meat bought at local markets; however, he was clear to say, "I did not eat sheep meat . . . hated it, and still do." He remembers that in Texas, the Angora goat ranchers provided meat for the shearers; it was a tradition around the Brackettville area. "That meat I did eat," he said.

In Texas he sheared with other captains, including Gregorio Talamantes, Belio Villarreal of Rocksprings, Chago Uriegas of San Angelo, and Moises Reyes of Uvalde. Some shearers he sheared with from Brackettville were Pache Samaniego, Ramon Garcia, Pablo Garcia, and Adrian Reyes. He remembered that the great shearers, *las sorgas* as he calls them, from Brackettville were Tana Peña and Fito Garcia. He said that Garcia was a thin man, but "que alma de hombre para trasquilar" (what a soul he had for shearing).

After some forty-nine years, Felipe stopped working as a shearer in 1985. He then started his own shearing crew and had *ocho manos* (eight hands, or shearers). His shearers were mostly from Brackettville, but he did hire some from Mexico. He told me the men from Mexico were *muy buena gente* (really good people). He said, "They came to work and did not complain, and we trusted them with reganche." He further explained, "No heran reglistas" (They were not complainers).

I asked him about some memories he had of shearing. Interestingly, he did not remember the hard times; rather, he told me a story of good times, and he laughed heartily the whole time. The story went that one of the shearers by the last name of Botello had developed a bad stomach ailment. He asked the captain to take him to the doctor, but the captain refused. He said, "Just give him some remedio [home remedy] and he will be fine." However, the man just could not heal. He kept saying his stomach was feeling so bad that he preferred to die rather than feel so bad. This continued for about three days as the sick man kept saying he wanted to die. Finally a shearing companion, exhausted of the belly-aching (literally!) found his pistol, took three bullets, and removed the lead from the shells (Felipe remembered that they all carried guns at the time). The shearing companion refilled the shells with hardened goat grease and reloaded them in his pistol. Sure enough, the sick man again still said he wanted to die. The companion took out his gun and said, "Okay, let me help you." He shot the man three times in the chest with the goat-grease-filled bullets. The sick man spread out his arms and screamed, "I don't want to die!" The next day he was fine, except for some deep bruises on his chest. They later realized that the sick man just did not want to shear, so he pretended to be sick. Felipe laughed heartily at the memory.

Felipe tells another tale of a rancher who warned them not to mess with his turkeys. Subsequently one of the laneros was pranked into preparing one of the birds for breakfast. And of course, the entire crew was run off the ranch.

We ended the interview as Felipe lamented the fact that he knew of no shearing still going on in the Brackettville area. He said he raised his family of fourteen with la trasquila. They did not have much, but they always had enough to be happy as a family, he said. La trasquila was hard work, he continued. But if you worked hard, you could make a good living doing the work.

Felipe lived alone, but his daughter Terry saw him every day. He continued to read the Bible and ask the good Lord to let him live to be one hundred. However, Felipe Martinez died in November 2021; he was two weeks from his ninety-ninth birthday. He is interred at the Brackettville cemetery.

9

Los Rancheros
The Ranchers

As one reads about the origins and developments of the Angora goats in Texas, a rich history of success is evident. It is also evident that there are many notable families in Texas who were instrumental to the success of its ranching and shearing industries. Indeed, it would require an entire book, at least, to do justice to their histories.

O. C. Fisher and Lem Jones created excellent lists and wrote of the rich histories of hundreds of Texas ranching families and their efforts to raise Angora goats and sheep. The stories are very informative and chronicle especially well the importation and gradual development of the Angora goat in Texas. This chapter documents three of those families through personal interviews: the Earwoods, the Davises, and the Rosses. They are the families who, according to longtime Angora goat rancher Joe David Ross, have "the longest history of raising Angora goats in Texas." The interviews did not concentrate solely on shearing; rather, it was important to capture the larger stories of the families since they were and remain extremely important to the sheep and Angora goat industry. However, their stories are also relevant to the shearing industry because, as Ross said, "Shearing could not exist without the ranchers, but Angora goat ranching could not exist without the shearers."

This chapter offers brief vignettes of three families who were involved in the beginnings, struggles, challenges, and highlights of sheep and goat ranching in Texas. The interviewees give us hope that the sheep and Angora goat ranching and shearing industries will continue in some fashion.

Edward Armer Earwood

The interview was conducted at the Earwood Ranch, located south of Sonora. A part of the day was spent admiring some of Edward Earwood's Angora nannies and billy goats. Leo, Edward's Border Collie dog, reacted to a "way 'round" order and brought to the pen some billy goats for a closer look.

Many shearing memories came flooding back as Edward also showed me the shearing shed that they had used over the years. It was one where the captain could readily move the shearing trailer in, set up, and start shearing in just a few minutes. Even the smells associated with shearing were still there. The table where the mohair was collected was still in the shed, as was the packing frame. Edward's wife, Pam, treated us to a delicious lunch, and we then sat down to talk about ranching and the shearing industry.

In discussing the beginnings of the Earwood family ranch and the family's involvement with sheep and goats, Edward indicated that it

Edward and Pam Earwood, Earwood Ranch, October 2020. Photograph from author's collection.

Earwood registered Angora billy goats, Earwood Ranch, October 2020. Photograph from author's collection.

came from both the paternal and maternal sides of his family. Edward's great-great-grandfather, John Washington Putnam, began homesteading a piece of land some thirty miles south of Sonora prior to 1901. In 1901 John Putnam finalized the paperwork with the State of Texas, and soon thereafter the land was deeded to his daughter, Sara Joanna, "Johnnie Annie"; and son-in-law, George Clyde, "G. C.," Earwood, thus creating the ranch now known as the Earwood Ranch.

According to Edward, George Clyde started the tradition of raising Angora goats on the Earwood side of the family and developed his herd to a fine quality, so much so that many Angora goat breeders came from great distances to buy his goats. George Clyde and Johnnie Annie had nine children: five girls and four boys. Edward's grandfather, Fred Earwood, was one of the sons. Fred began ranching with his father as a young boy and soon started his herd of Angora goats by purchasing some registered goats from his father. Keeping track of the sire and dams enabled Fred to further improve his goat herd.

On the other side of the family, Margaret Reid Armer was Edward's great-grandmother, living in Kingston, New Mexico. Margaret Reid's first husband died of typhoid fever, leaving her with six children. Margaret purchased her first Angora goat in 1887, and the goats became the life-blood for Margaret and her children by providing meat, milk, and fiber for the family. The goats also provided income as Margaret sold fiber, milk, cheese, and an occasional kid goat. Margaret later married Leven Edward Armer in 1894, and together they had three children. Leven was an engineer by trade and soon built a steam-driven shearing machine for his wife to help the shearing go easier. Previously the shearing had been done by hand.

Margaret Reid Armer was so successful with her Angora goats in New Mexico that she became known as the "Angora Goat Queen." She showed and won many prizes with her champion goats in several state fairs around the United States. O .C. Fisher (1985) wrote extensively about Margaret, extending her title to "The Angora Queen of America," justifiably so, since Margaret, in addition to having champion goats, at one time marketed twenty-five thousand pounds of mohair at fifty to eight-five cents per pound. Edward's grandmother, Mary Annette Armer, was the daughter of Margaret Reid and Leven Armer.

Edward's grandfather Fred Earwood spent his life on the Earwood Ranch. Fred had some good goats on the ranch, but he wanted to improve their quality. Author Lem Jones noted that Fred had bought his first goats from his own father, George Clyde Earwood, in 1918 and became one of the most prominent goat men in the United States. When Fred married Mary Armer of New Mexico in 1920, they formed what Jones called "an Angora goat dynasty that continues to this day" (1995).

How that marriage of 1920 came to be is a story that is surely unique among ranchers. Fred had heard of the Armer family having good-quality goats in New Mexico, so he decided to make a trip to see if he could buy some. The Fred and Mary romance began somewhat by chance at first sight. Mary was separating goats through a chute when Fred first saw her. However, not only did her looks capture him, but when he noticed she was separating the goats in three ways through the cutting chute and at the same time counting one of the separated groups, he knew she was the one he wanted to marry. After all, anyone knows that cutting and separating goats through a chute two ways is a difficult task, but managing them three ways is really impressive. Fred knew it required a real goat man—or, rather, woman—to do so.

Edward says that Fred Earwood and others also established the Sonora Wool and Mohair Company. As Fred dealt with buyers through his

Mary, Fred, and son Armer Earwood, 1925. Photograph courtesy of Edward Earwood.

work at the warehouse, it became obvious to him that ranchers needed to be selective in the breeding of their goats to have better mohair. From these observations Fred became a leader in developing high-quality wool and mohair and became known as "Mr. Sheep and Goat Raiser." He understood well what the buyers wanted. Grandmother Mary worked alongside him at the ranch and the warehouse, so together they spent their lives helping people raise better goats and obtain better mohair. According to Edward, Fred was also hailed when he was a member of the delegation that went to Washington, D.C., to advocate for the Wool Act of 1954. The delegation was successful, as the act became law soon thereafter.

Mary Armer Earwood, Edward's grandmother, lived to be ninety-four years old and spent practically all of her time on the Earwood Ranch. She worked extremely hard during kidding time, and other than her family, that was her love. She was not one to prize luxuries, but she enjoyed working with her goats.

Edward's father, Armer Earwood, and his mother, Barbara Tirrell Earwood, were married in 1942 and had three children: Elsie, Melinda, and Edward. Armer was born in Del Rio in 1921 and was an only child.

Early on he attended school in Sonora but only through the first grade. Later a teacher was hired to teach him at the ranch from second grade through junior high school. He then attended the Texas Military Institute (TMI) in San Antonio and then the University of Texas at Austin.

Armer and Barbara's romance and marriage also had a unique beginning. After returning to the ranch in Sonora, Armer had become friends with the son of a wool buyer. In those days all the wool from Sonora was shipped to Boston, Massachusetts. In Boston the wool was scoured and turned into fabric and yarn. As Edward tells it, Armer was interested in finding out the final destination of wool shipped from the Earwood Ranch. Armer and a friend boarded a train to the Texas coast and then a ship to Boston harbor. The wool buyer who had bought the Sonora wool also had his own scouring plant. Armer stayed for about a month to observe how the scouring process was done.

While attending church one day in Weymouth, a suburb of Boston, Armer met his future bride, Barbara Tirrell. They dated for about a year via letters written back and forth. Barbara came to visit the ranch in Texas before getting married, and she fell in love with it. She became a Texan and always thanked Armer for "saving her from a life in the city." The couple lived for a while in Culberson County and raised sheep and goats.

Keeping up with the records of Angora goat sires, nannies, and kid goats was a labor-intensive effort for Fred's father. Goat numbers were limited because the goats were registered and the labor needed to keep straight records of the sires and dams of each kid was extensive. However, Armer and Barbara kept the numbers to about typically two thousand sheep and two thousand Angora goats.

When asked about his own early involvement with raising Angora goats, Edward responded, "I can't even remember not being involved with goats. As a toddler and young boy I was always with my father working goats. In 1968 when my grandfather passed away, I was about seven years old, so I did not get to know him as well as my grandmother." The kidding season for registered Angora goats is always a lot of work. Kids have to be marked to their nannies, their survival has to be monitored, and much more. It was during those times that Edward was always with his dad working with goats. "Rancher is what I am," was the response when asked about his occupation. As such, Edward did not

Earwood registered nanny Angora goats, Earwood Ranch, October 2020. Photograph from author's collection .

feel like he ever truly owned his goats; rather, he felt more like he was the caregiver of Angora goats that were at the ranch and were handed to him from his ancestors.

Edward was born on May 26, 1961, in Sonora. He was the youngest child of the family, born when his mother was forty years old. At this time his dad was older and not feeling very well. So at the young age of twenty-three, Edward had the ranch turned over to him after he graduated from Angelo State University. His dad and he became partners in the Earwood Ranch. His dad was still actively involved in ranch matters, so Edward continued to learn as much as he could. Edward remembers that his dad was very forgiving and willing to try all of Edward's ideas as long as Armer's core method of ranching was continued. Edward stated, "I have such a great family history of ranchers that I am just trying to carry on the tradition." He has been at it all his life.

The interview conversation immediately lost its wistfulness as the discussion transitioned to Edward's memories about shearing season. His eyes lit up as he remembered that when the shearers arrived, it was almost like the circus arriving at the ranch: lots of trucks, different vehicles, and lots of activity; it was quite a festive time. He recalls that the shearing truck was a shearing rig that had the motor powering the drops and headpieces located on the truck itself. The motor on the truck had six drops on each side; therefore, it accommodated twelve shearers.

The most vivid memories were divulged as he remembered the cook who came with the shearing crew. Being able to speak fluent Spanish, Edward recalled well the cocinero. As a child it was always a treat for him to eat the cocinero's food, cooked over an open fire on the ground. He clearly remembered that at 3:00 p.m., everything shut down. The cocinero prepared an atole for all of the crew as they took their afternoon snack. The atole consisted of rice, milk, cinnamon, and brown sugar. The sweet atole was served in a coffee cup. One time the cook was stirring the pot and the young Edward asked about the "black things" in the atole. The cook replied in Spanish, "No te preocupes, nomas son moscas" (Don't worry about it, they are just flies). They were actually raisins!

He remembers that the cook prepared the pan de campo so well and it went perfectly with beans and goat meat. Edward indicated that he did not remember tortillas that much, but apparently the pan de campo was memorable, so much so that in later years Edward and Pam would bake it for hundreds of hunters who attended the annual Sonora hunter's festival.

Asked about the meat being the main dish for the shearing crews, Edward recalled that his father provided the meat from some of their own billy kids. Providing meat for the shearers was an age-old tradition, and Edward said that his dad always followed that tradition. Currently, shearers do not stay as long, but Edward and Pam still provide a meal for them. Edward became pensive as he said that there was something very special about working and eating together. The camaraderie developed during those times was memorable.

There was still one more great memory to share before leaving the subject. Edward recalled the shearing seasons. His father always kept some Jersey milk cows on the ranch. He had also obtained a Jersey bull that was used to breed the cows. The shearers always camped out under a grove of live oaks close to the shearing pens. At night they would set out their cots under the trees, but not too close to each other; apparently the snoring was so bad that the cots had to be a good distance apart. It just so happened that the Jersey bull was kept in the same trap (small pasture) where the crew set their camp. During the dark and moonless night, the ever-mischievous (*travieso*, as Edward puts it) bull had some fun going around and flipping over one cot after another. In the dark night, the shearers did not know what had hit them. They ran around yelling, "La bruja! La bruja!" (The witch! The witch!).

Edward also remembered some of the crews that came to shear their sheep and goats. When he was a kid, Eddie Barrera's shearing crew out of Del Rio sheared their animals. That was his earliest memory of the crews, and they were the ones who had the truck with the shearing motor on top and the six drops on either side. Other crews stayed for one or two years, but he remembers the Eddie Franco crew out of Rocksprings and that Keno Falcon of Camp Wood sheared many years for him. Currently, Paco Ramirez of Rocksprings does his shearing. Edward said that Captain Ramirez takes only four or five shearers to the ranch these days, and it was evident to Edward that the shearers are older men. Edward is concerned that ranchers will not be able to find shearers in the future. "We cannot exist as Angora goat ranchers without the shearers," he said.

As we continued the interview, I asked my next question: "What are the highlights in your life as you work with Angora goats?"

The response was clearly heartfelt as he answered, "Honest to goodness, it is when my family, daughters, wife . . . when we can all work together to work the goats. When we are shearing, when the nannies are kidding, and even better now that I have my grandkids in the middle of everything, they are already wanting to be in the middle of everything, and that gives me great joy."

I asked, "Will you encourage your grandkids to raise Angora goats?"

"Absolutely!" he said. "Both of my daughters are ranchers; it is in our blood. There is something very unique about Angora goats; they have personality and steal your heart very quickly. Can't help but love them," he says.

As we delved into the future for Angora goats in general, Edward was somewhat skeptical. He said he wished he would live to see a resurgence in the Angora goat industry. "However, I am afraid I don't see it coming," he says. Edward feels that the decline stems mostly from the fact that all early fabrics came from natural fibers such as cotton, wool, and mohair. Mohair was made into a fabric that lasted forever, and one could own a coat that could even be passed down to others. Now there are synthetics that are cheaply made, and natural fibers cannot compete, price-wise. He continues, "I think it goes along with a throwaway attitude that seems to be prevalent in our society. Now people tend to buy things that are made to be disposable. I don't want to be pessimistic," he says, "but I see fewer and fewer goats. We used to sell a lot of billies to ranchers who wanted to use them to add quality to their herds, but I don't see it much anymore."

We concluded our interview with one last question. "With all its challenges, why do you still stay in the Angora goat ranching business?"

He answered, "It is my family heritage. All I know about Angora goats was taught to me by my grandfather and my father." He continues, "Angora goats are unique animals to work with, and I love to work with them. It is in my history, in my blood, bottom line. More than tradition … more like in my DNA." Edward closed by saying, "Shearing is an industry that is fading away, too. Its history needs to be recorded for the future so other generations can read about it."

His comment made me think of and appreciate more our lunchtime. We had lunch earlier in the day, and Edward asked that we say grace before our food. He blessed the food, and as part of the blessing he asked that I be given the strength to write my book.

Jad Davis

Jad Davis comes from the Davis family lineage, and it is necessary to capture his story since he represents the descendants of a long line of Angora goat ranchers dating back to the initial importation of Angora goats to the United States. John Allen Davis Jr., known to his family and friends as "Jad," sat down with me to discuss Angora goats. We had spent the better part of the day observing and taking pictures of his Angora

Jad Davis at the Davis Ranch cabin, October 2020. Photograph from author's collection.

goats at his Davis Ranch, located on Cherry Creek, halfway between Rio Frio and Utopia. The ranch has been in the family for well over one hundred years. It was a morning well spent, admiring some fine Angora goats, and it was now time to talk about them. We started out talking about Jad's predecessors.

He recalled that the first importation of Angora goats to the United States was actually tied to Jad's family. In 1849, James B. Davis brought Angora goats to the United States that had been gifted to him by the sultan of Turkey. This early importation eventually had an impact on Jad Davis's family, since James Davis was a cousin to John Henry Davis, Jad's great-grandfather.

The John Henry Davis family moved to Edwards County in 1888 and settled at the headwaters of the Nueces River; the area later became known as Vance. As Jad told it, according to Lora B. Davis Garrison, a daughter of John Henry, in that same year a cattle drive stopped in the Vance area and two calves were born. The calves, being too young to travel with the cattle drive, were given to the young Bob Davis, son of John Henry. The calves were later traded for eleven old Angora nanny goats owned by a Johnny Brown of Vance. However, Bob acquired a greater number of goats, as his uncle Nat Davis gave him thirty head as a reward for having taken care of his herd. Those goats from Nat Davis all had what was called an "underbit" ear notch. Nat Davis had acquired his first goats from James B. Davis. Thus, goats from James Davis went to Nat Davis, and from him to Bob Davis. It was through this chain of events that the underbit Angoras became part of the legacy of the Davis Angora goats and where the Davises' long and strong ties to the Angora goat industry began.

Robert Franklin "Bob" Davis was born in Brown County in 1880. He was the son of John Henry Davis and Nancy Susan Blanton Davis. The goats received in trade for the calves, plus the thirty goats given to Bob by his uncle Nat, would eventually lead to the development of a herd of goats that would be recognized internationally.

Jad tells a great story about Bob, his grandfather. At the age of eighteen, Bob had met Annie Auld at a dance. She was younger than he, but, there being few girls to dance with, he danced with the then twelve-year-old Annie. However, before that dance was over, Bob told Annie that when she was old enough, he was going to marry her. As the years passed and after many nights visiting on the porch, playing dominos, and being around each other at different times, Bob and Annie agreed to marry. Bob was now twenty-three and Annie, eighteen. When Bob asked for Annie's hand in marriage, her father, Alex Auld, who had come from Scotland, wanted to adhere to traditional Scottish ways. Those traditions and customs called for the older daughter to get married before the younger daughter could. So the response to Bob's wedding request was, "No, but you can marry Dolly, who is the oldest daughter." As the story goes, Bob said, "No, I'm in love with Annie." The answer was still a strong, no! So, as many star-crossed lovers do, Bob and Annie eloped. They agreed to the time and place, and Bob brought to the rendezvous point two horses. They rode off to Leakey, where a Judge Sansom then promptly married Bob and Annie in October 1903.

However, Annie Auld, Bob's wife and later Jad's grandmother, also had an auspicious story for her beginnings. Alex Auld lost his brother while he was still young. His brother had come with him from Scotland, and they had been together as they became Americans. Alex's brother became ill and returned to Scotland, where he passed away not long afterward. Having lost his brother and now being alone, Alex felt he needed to marry. He went to Kerrville and met with Captain Schreiner, a renowned citizen of Kerrville at the time, to ask if the captain could help find him a ranch wife. Schreiner said that in fact, he knew a widow who had lost her husband after he had died from being kicked in the head by a horse. Alex Auld and the widow Susanna Lorance, who had one young daughter, were introduced, and after three days of courting, he asked her to marry him. They married and moved to the Auld Ranch. Billie Jean Davis, Jad's mother, recounts that the widow Lorance was a real ranch woman. She gave birth to Annie, Maggie, John, Archie, Willie, Dan, and Marcus, all the while running the ranch.

Alex Auld had been an engineer in Scotland. The fences he built on the ranch were in the Scottish fashion of stacked stones. When the Schreiner Hospital was built in Kerrville, the stones from those fences were donated and used to construct the front wall of the hospital. So from that Auld-Lorrance family came Annie, who married Bob. Bob and Annie's family would later include eight children: Arthur, Henry, Susie, Wesley, Zylpha, Bob Jr., Lora B., and John Allen. All of the children except John Allen were born on the Cherry Creek Ranch.

The Cherry Creek Ranch came about in 1908, when Bob and Annie Davis bought the Arthur Kelley Survey homestead, which comprised 640 acres. The ranch was located adjacent to Cherry Creek in Uvalde County. The couple traded a team, a wagon, and other items for the ranch. When they settled in, Bob and Annie brought with them their underbit Angora goats. According to Jad, the Davis Ranch increased in size over the years and was as large as four thousand acres at one time, large enough to support a herd of twenty-five hundred Angora goats. Bob Davis died in 1960, but Grandmother Annie lived to be ninety-four years old and lived on the ranch.

Bob and Annie's youngest son was John Allen Davis Sr., Jad's father. John Allen Davis Sr. married Billie Jean Faulkner in Leakey in August 1952. Billie Jean and John Allen were both from the Frio River Canyon and attended the Leakey public schools. They had a daughter, Teralea, and John Allen Jr., "Jad." John Allen Sr. was the superintendent of schools for the Nueces Canyon school district in Barksdale and later became the dean of student services at Southwest Texas Junior College, where he worked until his retirement. Billie Jean was a schoolteacher and counselor for the Uvalde ISD for many years. She was present for Jad's interview in October 2020.

John Allen Sr. kept the family tradition alive and well as he took over the Davis Ranch and continued to raise Angora goats. Upon his death, he left the ranch to Jad and Teralea Davis Jones as co-owners. Their agreement was that Jad now would run the place, make improvements, and keep the Angora goats with lineage to the original goats brought on the property. Teralea supports his efforts 100 percent, according to Jad.

Jad was born February 21, 1957, in Fort Benton, Georgia, since his dad was in the military at the time. However, as Jad puts it, "He got back to Texas as quickly as he could." Jad proudly regards himself as an eighth-generation Texan. During Jad's early childhood years, his family lived near Vance and then moved to Montell, where they lived on a ranch leased by his father. Jad was in the sixth grade when they once again moved, this time to Fourth Street in Uvalde. To this day he remembers being heartbroken when they left Nueces Canyon and so many close friends. However, he adjusted to Uvalde, became a stellar student and football player, and managed to visit the Davis Ranch as often as possible. He graduated from Uvalde High School and then attended Southwest

Texas Junior College in Uvalde. From there he transferred to Texas A&M University in College Station and earned a bachelor's degree. Law school came next, as he was accepted to the Baylor College of Law in Waco. When visiting with Joe David Ross in Sonora, I mentioned that I would be interviewing Jad Davis. Joe David said, "You do know Jad is a famous lawyer, right?"

After graduation from law school, Jad moved to Midland and began to practice law. It was also in the busy year of 1982 when he married his wife of thirty-eight years, Carla Jacob Davis. They have three children: John Jacob, Kyle Allen, and Kali Ann. They also now have five grandchildren: Case, Emma, Campbell, Annie, and Bradford.

As we visited on that October day, Jad added another story to the original acquisition of the Angora goats by Bob Davis, his grandfather. One story tells that the goats supposedly went to California via ship from New Orleans around South America. Another story has it that the goats were actually driven across land to the West Coast. Nevertheless, when Nat got older, he brought the goats overland from California to Vance, where young Bob tended them and was given thirty goats as payment for his work. He was told he could pick out the ones he wanted to keep. Having tended the goats for some time, Bob knew which ones were the pick of the litter. That bloodline of goats was brought to the Cherry Creek Ranch in 1908, and the underbit goats were always marked separately.

As Angora goats increased in numbers in the area and in Texas in general, a strong effort was made to develop a registration system. Bob Davis proposed to the registration administrators that one hundred of his best underbit nannies be registered, and they were all accepted for registration. The now-pedigreed one hundred nannies were his first group of registered goats. Angora goat pedigrees for the Davis registered goats have been kept since.

Davis developed a much better stock of registered Angora goats from that group of one hundred. In 1921, Bob bought an Angora buck (billy goat) from John Allen Ward of Sonora for $3,080, an unheard-of amount of money at that time. Thus, the "John Allen" name was introduced into the Davis family, as Bob and Annie's youngest child was named after John Allen Ward.

Jad is proud of his Angora goats. He says that he has never bought an outside nanny goat; his goats all have some degree of Davis lineage. Jad recounts one of the great, yet sad stories behind that lineage. According to Jad, Bob and Annie at one time had one thousand nanny goats that had given birth to about five hundred kids. In those days it was a well-known and well-used practice to tie the kid goats to a stake until they got old enough to follow the nannies out to pasture. The nannies were set loose during the day so they could feed and then came back in the afternoon to their staked-out kids. So the nannies were set out to graze across Cherry Creek on that memorable day. A strong rain came during the day, and the freshly sheared nannies were all lost to the flooded Cherry Creek: a huge "die-out" as termed by goat ranchers. The kid goats were all sure to die of starvation, so they were mercifully put out of their misery.

However, about fifteen or twenty kid goats were kept, and Annie bought an extra milk cow and bottle-fed them. Arthur, Bob's brother, raised some of those kids and added them to his Davis bloodline; however, he was later killed in a tractor accident. Not long after that, Arthur's widow, Aline, gifted Jad and his father three old nannies; those nannies were from the original Davis bloodline. The nannies were old, but John Allen Sr. fed them oatmeal. The first kidding season, two of the nannies had billy kids, but one nanny had twin nanny kids. The nanny kids were kept and raised. The next season the old nanny was bred again and had more kids. Most important, the original lineage from the original importation of Angora goats to the United States was salvaged. He proudly has kept the Davis Angora goat lineage that can be traced and documented back to nanny number 6045, which was given to them by Aline Davis from Arthur Davis's goats, from the original underbit Davis goats.

Jad could not recall if it was a Texas Angora Goat Raisers Association (TAGRA) meeting or not, but a huge event was held in Camp Wood in the 1920s. Jad related the story that registered Angora goats were brought from South Africa, and a big sale was held in Camp Wood on that day. One fellow was extremely proud that he was able to buy a South African billy goat of such perceived quality that it even had mohair on its tail: something extraordinary at the time and something no one had ever seen in Texas. The fellow was so proud of his acquisition that he kept bragging about and showing the goat to anyone who would listen. That night some young boys found hand shears and clipped all the hair off the goat's tail so that it looked like a rat's tail. The next morning the fellow was still showing off the goat, but minus the hair on its tail. To this day, many Angora goat breeders refer to goats with no mohair on their tail as "a rat-tailed goat." Jad still laughs heartily at the story passed down to him and suspects it was one of his uncles who did the "shearing."

At this point we turned the conversation to shearers he had known over the years. Jimmy Balderas Sr. and Isabel "Chavel" Sanchez came to mind as he bemoaned the slow disappearance of shearers, which he said has become a factor affecting the goat industry.

Jad related that the Angora goat business did well in the early days due to mohair being used in Model A car seats, movie theater seats,

Davis Angora nanny goats with Jad Davis in background, Davis Ranch, October 2020. Photograph from author's collection.

and movie theater curtains. He also said, "If we can somehow create that type of universal use again, we could perhaps see a resurgence in the business. For example, the universal use of mohair in carpeting at airports is taking hold, because the mohair lasts so long, even in heavy foot traffic." He added, "The cottage industry for the mohair fabric is also promising, but small. Maybe natural fiber and environmental benefits will lead to a resurgence," he concluded.

Jad keeps a record of nannies and how many kids they have had, how old the nannies are, the quality of hair they produce, and all other variables that come into play to develop exceptional registered goats. He further says, "The billies I keep are out of nannies with impeccable performance."

However, his results have not come about quickly. After trying to develop fine Angora goats for about thirty years without compromising conformation and shearing weight, Jad was just not seeing good results. He considered that as one of his most challenging times and a low point in his Angora goat career. However, he kept trying to get good-bodied, fine-haired goats. He had big goats that he sheared a lot, but he would compete in the TAGRA shows and none of his goats were ever picked as

Davis registered Angora billy goat, Davis Ranch, October 2020. Photograph from author's collection.

Isabel "Chavel" Sanchez shearing the Davis Angora bucks, Davis Ranch, summer 2018. Photograph courtesy of Jad Davis.

Jad's grandson, Bradford Davis, in the shearing pen with shearer Juan Gonzales of Camp Wood, Davis Ranch, summer 2019. Photograph courtesy of Jad Davis.

winners; they just did not sell. After thirty years of development, he felt his goats were not getting better. However, he kept culling, kept the best of the best, and eventually it paid off. In 2019, one hundred years after his grandfather helped start TAGRA, Jad had a boom year. He had the first-, second-, and third-place sales bucks. His first-place Angora buck was also designated as the Grand Champion goat of the show and sale. In 2020, he again had the first-, second-, and third-place sales bucks. All of those bucks were from the same "outlier" buck Jad had raised and is still breeding.

The last and perhaps most difficult question posed was, "Although you are now a successful attorney and live hundreds of miles away from the Cherry Creek Ranch, why do you stay in the Angora goat business?"

He answered, "It is almost my worldview since being a young boy: a world where neighbors all know each other, and when it came time to get together, it was to attend church, to round up, to shear, to drench, and to work the goats in general. Many friends and families came together to help." Jad continued, "I always wanted to be a good man to my family and neighbors. Secondly, my heroes were always goat ranchers. People such as the Rogerses, the Ewings, Teagues, Lockharts, and of course the Davises and other families who raised Angora goats were my heroes. They were all intertwined in their history of working in the Angora goat industry. To this day, they still pursue the idea of having the best goats."

Davis ranch sign, October 2020. Photograph from author's collection.

He added, "I have done it all my life; my family has, too. The thought of not having goats has never crossed my mind. I like being around goat people, the industry, the friends, the culture."

After the interview and as I left Jad's ranch that day, I had to capture one last photograph: the sign hanging at the entrance to his ranch. It proudly portrays the finest billy goat Jad has raised to date, billy number 861. Most important, that sign cites the year the ranch on Cherry Creek was established, 1908. That sign again reminded me why Jad's story was important. He represents the descendants of a long line of Angora goat ranchers dating back to the initial importation of Angora goats to the United States.

Joe David Ross

The next rancher interview conducted was with the elder statesman of the group, Joe David Ross. Joe David also comes from a long line of Angora goat ranchers. By profession he has been a doctor of veterinary medicine, but at heart he is a goat rancher. He was born to Joe Brown Ross and Lena Belle Briggs Ross on August 6, 1935, in Pearsall. His birth happened to be in Pearsall because his dad was pasturing cattle in the Dilley area during the drought years of the 1930s and 1940s. However,

Joe David and son David Lee Ross, near Sonora, circa 2012. Photograph courtesy of Joe David Ross.

not long after Joe David's birth, the Ross family moved back to the ranch in Sonora.

His parents met at Southwestern University in Georgetown in the 1920s. Joe was from Sonora, and Lena Belle was from Lampasas. Lena Belle became a schoolteacher, but their hearts were in ranching, and thus they settled in Sonora. They arrived there right before the Great Depression and ultimately lived through some hard times, including World War II and the drought years of the 1950s. However, they survived to raise a family of three, including Kathryn, Joe David, and Betsy. Those three children represented the third generation of Rosses who worked with Angora goats.

As a third-generation goat rancher, Joe David admits that his love and passion for Angora goats came from his grandfather Joe N. Ross. Joe N. had a fourth-grade education but was a pioneer in the true sense of the word. He had come to Llano from Arkansas with his family but then was orphaned. A saloon owner helped the children by giving Joe N. a job at the saloon, and Joe N. became a pool shark by the age of fifteen. According to Joe David, the bartender would set up cowboys to play against the young Joe N. With a wink from the bartender, Joe N. would promptly run the table.

Seeking a better life for himself, Joe N. and his three siblings joined a wagon train from Fort Worth that was going south to Vance, located in the Hill Country between Uvalde and Rocksprings. Joe N. met Kate on the wagon train, and they were married in the late 1880s. They worked on the Brown Ranch near Vance and eventually accumulated some Angora goats of their own. The pioneer spirit once again took hold, and in 1892, Joe N. and Kate herded their Angoras north, where they homesteaded several sections of land eighteen miles east of Sonora. The ranch has remained in the family since that day. Times on the ranch were not always good. Joe N. once lost half of his five thousand Angora goats to a cold rain that came right after shearing (Fisher 1985).

Joe David also recounted a story about his grandfather almost losing the ranch. An out-of-town loan officer had come to collect a debt that Joe N. had secured by using the Ross Ranch as collateral. Joe N. had five years of mohair in storage from the five thousand goats he had sheared over five seasons, but mohair was worth six cents per pound. Joe N., however, was adamant: "No, you are not taking my mohair, because even if we sell it at six cents, we are still broke." They hung on for six months until mohair prices increased to fifty cents per pound. The mohair was sold at that price, and the ranch survived. Kate Brown Ross passed away in 1920, and Joe N. died in 1938. Joe David still remembered his mother often telling him, "Don't ever forget that Angora goats saved this ranch." Joe David's mother died at the age of ninety-nine in 2003, but Joe David still remembers and lives by her words, and their goats persist.

The Joe David Ross family started in 1965 when he married Frances Koy Childress of Ozona; they have been married for fifty-five years and have three children: Joe Will, David Lee, and Mary Kathryn. All three still live close to Joe David and Frances and help the family in different ways.

Joe David's formal career began when he became a veterinarian after graduating from Texas A&M University in 1959. His practice was primarily with large animals. In 1969, Joe David's father passed away after a brief battle with cancer, and Joe David took complete control of their ranch. Wanting to be at home more with his three young children, he made the decision to do much less vet work and more ranching. However, he did not fully retire from doing vet work, as he continued to serve on several statewide committees and received appointments to various organizations representing the sheep and goat industry.

From 1970 through 1986, he served on the original Angelo Community Hospital Board. The National Minor Species Drug Use Committee was a major appointment for Joe David; however, his appointment to serve on the Texas A&M Foundation Board in 1981 was deeply meaningful. About forty members were appointed, and they met twice a year, doing work in oceanography, engineering, chemistry, human health, agriculture, and veterinary medicine. He worked on both state issues and national concerns. Joe David also worked with the Haby, Lockhart, Ross, and Speck team who imported their first group of South African Angora and Boer goats in 1991. One of the driving forces was to bring in new genetics. Long staple length, lower hemp levels, and a large, thick body on Angora goats in the United States have resulted from their efforts.

At the time of the interview in 2020, Joe David was eighty-five years old, and his mind and memory were as clear and vivid as ever. He first said that other than his family, his love and passion was raising Angora goats and trying to improve the land. He also used to raise sheep but recently sold them. Interestingly, he says he sold the sheep because of the excessive numbers of axis deer. When his pastures were intended to rest from grazing for 65 to 150 days so that the land and grass would recover in their rotational grazing system, axis deer jumped the fences into the pastures and ate the young grasses.

Joe David Ross holding daughter, Mary. On display is one of their champion Angora billy goats, circa 1972. Photograph courtesy of Joe David Ross.

Mohair and Angora goats have always been important to Joe David. He has kept as many as three thousand goats, along with sheep and cattle, at one time or another on the ranch. He thinks that Angora goats had the least severe impact on the land, since their eating habits were diversified and they were smaller than the meat goats "if you don't overstock," he says.

Joe David began culling his Angora goats much more carefully in 1969. He was still pleased with the fine hair being produced by his Angora goats, but as he carefully examined at least eight hundred nanny goats one day, his observations were that he needed to make some improvements. He remembered his vet days as dairy farmers commented, "Give reasonable care to all of your herd, but don't waste too much time on the lesser offspring and dogies." He also studied his father's records of their goats and found, going back at least ten years, that some bloodlines had fewer aborted Angora kids than others and that kids born in a barn had different responses to nursing without assistance. That kind of attention to developing quality Angora goats led to the fine herds he has owned.

Joe David's memory of shearing days include being four years old and being given the task of picking up the strands of mohair that floated loose in the shearing pens. He also recalls teaching his children to grade mohair. They at one time graded mohair into fifteen separate classes, just as done in South Africa, where Angora goats abound. Joe David's lesson to his children was that to compete with South African mohair, you have to grade mohair to perfection.

Joe David also recalled the Esau Ramirez shearing crew from Sonora, who sheared the Ross Angoras for over thirty years. The prices were well under one dollar per head in his early ranching days but now are four dollars or more per head and double for bucks. He recalled an early memory of seeing a crew of nineteen shearers on each side of the machine. There had to have been thousands of goats on the ranches to keep all those men busy. Joe David said that on his ranch there were typically eight to ten shearers total on the crews. They would shear well over a hundred goats each. He laments that now, due to the age of the shearers or just fewer goats, the men shear only forty to fifty per day.

On his ranch, Joe David also followed the age-old tradition of providing meat for the crews, and he still provides a goat when they are finished shearing on his ranch. Joe David says that he also now has to pay for the lanero and the empacador, whereas it used to be an expenditure borne by the captain.

The talk of memories led Joe David to believe that we will probably never again see the great days when Angora goats numbered in the millions. "It will be difficult to ever build up to any significant numbers," he says. "Fragmentation of the land, labor shortages, and predation, among other things, will make it difficult to achieve those numbers again." However, Joe David believes that mohair demand will always exist to some degree. He said, "Mohair adheres beautifully to dyes and is ever being blended with other materials to produce beautiful rugs, clothing, and other garments. It has never been as well-known as wool or cashmere, but it has its place. Mohair is a strong fiber, fire resistant, and blends well with other fibers, and this promises more value in the future."

I asked what he would advise people wanting to get into the business of raising Angora goats. He said, "Start with a small group of Angora goats. You could keep them in a barn at night or during bad weather, and they will survive." He adds, "Good net-wire fencing is usually necessary too." He noted that as people are learning to shear their own goats, learning to spin their own mohair, and with the advent of using dogs to guard their goats, a new rancher can make raising goats worthwhile. He advised improving the control of some weeds and certain brush and to make connections with local veterinarians. He concluded, "The price of mohair has been higher in the past ten years. However, even in years when mohair will be of low value, good times usually follow."

I gave him my thanks for being an Angora goat rancher, and I left him with a thought that I had developed over my conversations with him. I said to him that ranchers like him had provided shearing work for so many of us for so many years, and that work helped our families survive. He said, "And vice-versa. We could not have stayed in business without shearers." His last comment made me reflect that indeed our histories as shearers and ranchers have always been intertwined. Perhaps more important for the industry, our futures as shearers and ranchers are still dependent on each other for both enterprises to survive.

Learning of the four generations of Rosses and their involvement in raising Angora goats gave me a great perspective of what the industry has gone through and how it has endured, and it gave me a glimpse of the future. Joe N., Joe Brown, and Joe David Ross represent three generations of Rosses who have been and remain involved in the Angora goat business, by now in three different centuries. Knowing that Joe Will Ross, David Lee, and Mary Kathryn, Joe David's children, are following in his footsteps is a good sign for the Angora goat business and la trasquila.

Summary of the Interviews

It was not entirely unexpected that the ranchers would express consistency on various topics. For instance, I informed the interviewees that in my research I had found that at one time there were millions of goats on the Edwards Plateau and that it is estimated that there are now only between eighty thousand to one hundred thousand goats left in the area. Thus, I asked their thoughts on the reasons for the decline. Their responses were instructive. First, they felt that most people blamed it on the legislative loss of the Wool Act of 1954, or Incentive Program, as they also called it. However, they cited other reasons. They thought that the decline had more to do with Angora goats requiring a lot of work. "Work is good for us, but working Angora goats requires much work, and many people just do not want to do it," one interviewee said.

The subdivision of ranches into smaller lots was another consistent reason cited for the decline of the Angora goat industry. They also thought that the option of raising animals such as Spanish and Boer goats and Dorper sheep is less complicated, since ranchers do not have to worry about shearing and other labor demands.

The interviewees also believed that predation had an effect on raising Angora goats and had added to the decline. The predators in livestock areas have changed in numbers and species. In the past, ranchers dealt mostly with a few bobcats, rarely any coyotes, and never any hogs. Now all those predators are numerous and can be devastating to goat herds. Hogs are terrible on lambs and kid goats, such that they can devastate goat numbers. Coyotes are the same; they kill even grown animals, and though it is largely assumed that coyotes or hogs go only after the weak animals, the fact is that they go after the best animals too. Jad Davis recalled losing almost all his herd of kid goats to coyotes when his ranch hand did not pen them at night as he should have.

Also cited was the fact that flying predators, which historically have not been numerous or destructive, are nevertheless on the rise. The caracara hawk, moving north from Mexico, has begun to invade the ranches in some Texas counties. Sometimes called a Mexican eagle, the caracara is actually a small, eagle-like raptor that is known to mostly eat carrion but is now apparently killing live animals.

Another factor cited in doing business was the cost of labor, feed prices having skyrocketed the last few years, and the cost of doing business in general. Additionally, labor shortages are severe. Ranch hands and shearers are hard to find.

Finally, there is the great cost of goat losses. Edward Earwood remembered one year, when they had drenched all of their kid goats and kids had a reaction to the drench medicine, combined with eating a certain weed. He recalls losing about 50 percent of the kid crop. He also noted losing goats to bad weather.

The three interviewees take great pride in the fact that they are still in the Angora goat industry. Being in the business for three to four generations, they just do not see themselves ever not being Angora goat ranchers. I asked what they saw as the best Angora goats these days. They all consistently listed the same characteristics. First, they mentioned nannies with size and good weight, since heavier, bigger nannies tend to have stronger, healthier kids, and more of them, and the attentiveness of the nannies to their young. They also noted that one should consider the nannie's udder structure. Second, they felt that ranchers must have a good, big billy goat. Fertility is of utmost importance in this respect. And to develop the best lineage of goats possible, ranchers must keep a record of the nannies and their production.

Moving the discussion to mohair, I asked the interviewees what they thought was the best-quality mohair. They all thought that the mohair needed to be fine, low in microns of fiber diameter, and somewhat high yielding, lower in lanolin than what was more typical to the Angoras of the past. In the days of the Incentive Program, which was paid by weight, ranchers wanted hair heavy with lanolin on the goat. They also said that the industry as a whole did not worry as much about quality in those days, since the idea was to sell more, heavier mohair. Now ranchers want fine hair with less lanolin to stay competitive with the market at large. In essence, quality hair production is the primary goal for Angora goat ranchers these days, and production of meat is a secondary benefit. Some billy kids that are not kept for breeding purposes are generally sold for consumption. Breeding for good and structurally sound goats gives you meat as a valuable by-product, according to the interviewees.

All three interviewees agreed that organizations such as the Texas Sheep and Goat Raisers Association (TSGRA), TAGRA, and the Mohair Council of America are valuable resources that will contribute to any industry achievements in the future.

These ranchers have seen great challenges, have met the challenges, and plan to stay in the Angora goat business. And very important, they will always need tasinques.

10

Epilogue
We Were Once Shearers

In Texas the shearing seasons are generally measured by the corte largo (long season) that lasts from February to the end of June and the corte chiquito (short season) that lasts from early July to the end of September. For me the shearing seasons started in 1957, when I was six years old. That year in May, my father took me with him to Belle Fourche, South Dakota. He and my uncle Tano Aguero co-owned a shearing crew of ten shearers who consisted of their brothers, brothers-in-law, nephews, and close friends of the family. The cooks were my grandmother and two aunts, and the laneros were a cousin and my brother. I went along as a tagalong without my mother. I was somewhat a lanero but for only one shearer, my uncle Hilario "Layo" Aguero. I say "somewhat" because I could quit anytime I wanted and often did, because my father was the contractor for the crew, and he took me with him to visit various ranches to set the contracts and the Aguero crew's arrival date at the ranches. However, my first full-time job in the northern states was during the summer of 1963 in Montana as a lanero on the Lico Reyes crew from Uvalde. I earned four dollars per day, but I got to see much of Montana as we sheared around Browning and Heart Butte.

I then followed the traditional ladder for developing shearers. I became a full-time lanero with my father's crew after he started his own crew. Later I went with my uncle Tano's crew to Loma Alta as a full-time lanero for two years at the ages of eleven and twelve. One year later in the summer of 1964, I became a full-fledged shearer at the age of thirteen.

As a shearer my corte largo ran only on weekends, during spring break, or on holidays such as Easter. Since I was a full-time student, those were the only times I could shear during that corte, and my mother, Margarita Balderas Aguero, was not about to let me drop out of school to become a full-time shearer.

Those days I sheared locally with captains who had small crews, such as Pepe Chavez, Chon Barron, my godfather Ben Carabajal Jr., Ernest De Leon, Javiel De Leon, Polo Nevarez, my godfather Gonzalo Aguilera, and Chano Falcon. However, when school let out for the summer every year in mid-May, I would make the long drive to Belle Fourche with my uncle Manuel "Gugo" Aguero or my brothers Manuel, "Paipe," and Leandro Jr., "El Borao." I would shear all of the remaining days of the month of May and all of June in Montana and South Dakota. We ordinarily stayed in Belle Fourche through the Fourth of July for the big rodeo celebration and then returned to Texas.

In my start as a shearer in 1964, I progressed from being an apprentice on my uncle Tano Aguero's crew in the summer to my first trip to South Dakota in 1965 and 1966 as a tasinque on the Frank Hidalgo crew of Camp Wood. I then became an experienced tasinque with the Nino Garduña crew in the years of 1967–73. In the beginning I earned eleven cents per head shearing Angora goats in Texas. In the northern states such as the Dakotas and Montana, I earned twenty-five cents per head. In the latter years of my shearing career, I earned thirty or thirty-five cents per head.

As well as the pay per head, the crew captains mentioned provided "room and board." We still laugh at the fact that the "room" was some barn on a ranch or under the open skies. The bed was our own bedroll. The "board" was all the goat or sheep meat you could eat, plus tortillas, beans, and potatoes. Dessert was usually a molasses taco, and coffee and water were always included. When the shearing season started in Texas and our first meals were oven-cooked goat meat, tortillas, and beans, we were overjoyed at how delicious they were. After about ten days of the same, we started thinking about hamburgers.

I am often questioned about how we could possibly sleep on hard floors or rocky ground. After a hard day's work, you sleep standing up, if necessary. Further, how could we eat the same meals over and over? I often tell the story told to me on a shearing crew. A young man just did not get hungry and did not eat much. He complained to his father about it, since he was losing weight. His dad said, "Take this axe and go cut down that large oak tree in our pasture. When you get to the center wood, take a piece of it and make a tea of it. Drink the tea, and the tea will give you a great appetite." The son came back before he even got to the center of the oak and was starving. Such was our sleep and hunger, and again, we often remembered it with a saying: "El apetito es el mejor cocinero, y el trabajo la mejor cama" (Appetite is the best cook, and work the best bed).

One great side benefit of traveling to all of those states was that I got to see a huge part of the beautiful heartland of America. I saw a lot of it from the back of a pickup truck, but I marveled at it no less. I marveled at its vastness and its resources. I marveled at its good people and its friendly towns. I have often thought that travel greatly influenced my thinking about careers and education. To be outside one's tiny world of Camp Wood, my hometown, allowed me to see greater possibilities and erased the fear of moving from one town to another as I went to college and as I found new jobs in different cities.

I also had occasion to shear sheep in South Dakota in 1972 with the Arturo Sanchez, "El Quadrado" (Square), crew out of Sonora. He was called "Square" because he was a giant of a man with a giant heart. My longest tenure, however, was with the Nino Garduña crew. We were all over Montana and South Dakota. I once wrote a letter to a friend and mailed it from Jordan, Montana; the town was so isolated she could not find it on a map. The sign at the entrance to town read, "Jordan . . . city furthest from any other city in the US."

Once back in Texas, I would begin shearing Angora goats with my uncle Octaviano "Tano" Aguero's crew and did so for nine years. There would be ten of us shearers, five on each side of the shearing trailers. In the 1960s the motor was in the center of the shearing trailer. That motor drove the pulleys located along the long steel bar that ran the length of the trailer. Shearers never wanted the station or drop in the middle, because the noise was deafening and the exhaust from the motor was always in your eyes. Being near the motor was indeed hot, loud, and smoky. As a beginner and not having any seniority, I always wound up by the motor.

The long days of summer spent on my uncle Tano's crew were memorable. We would begin about July 8 and shear at the John Dooley Ranch at Laguna. Little did I know then that I was shearing goats at almost the same place where Angora goats first came to Texas. Packing our bedrolls and toolboxes, we would then head to the Loma Alta area between Sonora and Del Rio, which are ninety-two miles apart. That area of Texas is rocky, brushy, and almost in the middle of nowhere, but a great place to raise Angora goats. That area of the Edwards Plateau had thousands of Angora goats during the peak days of Angora goat ranching and during the time in which I sheared for my uncle Tano. I don't know how many goats we sheared in the time I spent during the summers on his crew, but it had to be more than eighty thousand head per summer. The ranchers I knew only as the Whiteheads had four ranches where we spent at least twenty days and sheared at least fifteen hundred goats per day as a crew. And we were only one of the crews in the area; there were also crews from Sonora, Rocksprings, Brackettville, Uvalde, and Del Rio.

My summer with Uncle Tano would last from July 8 until two-a-days started for football and, during my college years, until I had to register for college classes. It was very hard, hot, and dirty work, but I made enough money for tuition, travel, room, and board for college. The "room and board" were much better in college, by the way. And while my college friends spoke of hating for the summer to end and not wanting to return to college, I loved it; my "vacation" was starting.

My last true days of shearing coincidently involved shearing for an education. I remember shearing goats for a week with the Leonard "Boy" Hernandez crew the week before I left for Penn State to begin my doctoral studies. One of those days I sheared 165 goats by 4:00 p.m. One of the shearers, Roberto "Tito" Falcon, kiddingly accused me of not having been to school that summer; rather, he said, "I think you have been shearing up north all summer." I earned enough gas and food money for the road trip to Penn State.

Working with my uncle Tano in the 1960s and early 1970s gave us some great times. After saving for college expenses, I also had money left over to attend some Tejano dances, which seemed to be the greatest form of entertainment for tasinques, as well as movies. Even before I was twenty-one, beer seemed to be the potion that fueled our dances and certainly some of our days after work at Loma Alta. The store was so secluded that IDs were never required. At my recent fiftieth high school class reunion, we spoke of beer drinking during our younger days. I casually informed my classmates that I had given up drinking beer in 1995. Of course, I was asked, "Why 1995?" I told them that in my Hispanic culture we are taught that the good Lord gives us an allocation of beer for our lifetime. . . . I drank up my allocation by 1995!

Beer indeed was the drink of choice for other dances where Chicano (now called Tejano) music was played. We sang in English and Spanish, sometimes at the same time. We listened to country-western music on station KVOU in Uvalde and rock music on KONA in Oklahoma City and KTSA out of San Antonio. However, when we celebrated our life events such as weddings or *quinceañeras*, Chicano music was the sound.

At the movies our heroes were the cinema cowboys such as John Wayne, Charlton Heston, and even Roy Rogers. On the other hand, at the Sunday night movies filmed in Mexico, our heroes were Tony Aguilar, Luis Aguilar, and Miguel Aceves Mejia. Those Spanish-language movies were shown at the Nueces Theater owned by L. J. Dean in Camp Wood.

We also played America's great games such as football, basketball, and baseball. Early on, we played the games in the street in front of Javiel De Leon's house in Camp Wood. Our cheerleader was Tia Maria De Leon, Javiel's wife, who always sat on the porch smoking her cigarettes; however, as an elderly lady her cheers generally were a few curse words asking us to get off her [expletive] street. In retrospect, I now see that we were bilingual, bicultural, and by God, all-American.

The Tejano dances were special, however. We danced in the American Legion Hall in Camp Wood with great happiness to the sounds of the groups Zavala, Los Imperiales, and even the Vindells. However, the great bands such as Little Joe y La Familia, Los Perales, Agustin Ramirez, and Sunny and the Sunliners came to the civic center in Uvalde. Apparently our generation was not the only one to enjoy what was seemingly the greatest form of entertainment for Hispanic/Mexican American shearers: going to the *bailes* (dances).

An author wrote of his youth and attending dances in West Texas. He remembers that in the 1940s and 1950s, dances were by invitation only for families who had young ladies of dancing age. The men had to pay for their *distintivos*: passes pinned to the coat lapel that served as tickets to the hall and the dance floor. Older women chaperoned the young girls, and kids ran and played all over the dance floor. There were no tables in the hall, but the chairs were reserved for the young ladies who were lined up along a wall. The author wrote,

For my peers, it was always a big thrill to dance the opening tune. As
soon as the band struck up the music, the boys would make a beeline
toward the girls "*a nombrar*" ("to partner," or call on a girl to dance). It
was understood that one could not ask a girl who was going steady to
dance the first dance. Protocol called for her to save the first dance for
her boyfriend and vice versa. The same rule applied to the last number.
. . . [It was] a wholesome and respectful form of entertainment, and
liquor was forbidden inside the dance room, especially during the years
of prohibition (Guerrero 1991, 51).

For those of us growing up in the Camp Wood, Rocksprings, and
Uvalde areas of Texas, dancing had its own culture. To be good at dancing, you had to know how to dance to polka, waltz, *bolero*, *cumbia*,
Texas two-step (country-western), rock, and sometimes even *guapango*
music. I remember attending a dance in Uvalde at the civic center where
the Johnny Canales band was playing. He challenged us to dance to a
polka, which we did; then rock, which we did; then the Twist (that one
was easy). Then came a *cumbia*, to which we all heartily danced. Finally
he played a *guapango* (a sort of Mexican hat dance), and we danced to
that, too. He finally gave up and said, "Si asi fueran pa trabajar" (If only
you could work like that). Everyone broke out into laughter.

However, there were risks, too. At the dances, the young men stood
at a certain place in the hall, usually by the entrance. The girls sat on
long benches or chairs lined up next to the dance floor. To ask a girl to
dance, you had to walk the long and lonely distance to where the girls
were. If she said no, it was a long, embarrassing, and lonely walk back
to where the young men congregated. Of course, there was always the
loudmouth who would yell at you, "Estas muy feo!" (You are too ugly!).
The second risk was from the fights that seemed to always occur at the
dances. Some were serious, but most were just fist skirmishes. The dance
was evaluated the next day by how many fights had occurred. The more
fights, the better the dance had been.

Perhaps they were challenging times for adolescents during those
years, but many romances and eventual weddings were hatched at those
great bailes. The movies and dancing were indeed significant forms of
entertainment for us. They added to the great times we lived in as we
were young and as we were tasinques.

Shearing sheep and goats was hard work, but it did provide opportunities for us as young men. During our high school and college days and during the long seasons in Texas, many of us sheared on weekends, often on the Javiel De Leon crew, which consisted of eight stations/drops. During the week he was the captain of his crew, but by then it was only he and his two sons, Baldemar and Aurelio Sr. However, on the weekends he would employ eight of us students as his shearers. We went on to continue our education, and two of us earned doctoral degrees; three, master's degrees; and one, a bachelor's degree. One other shearer started his own company, but the other one was in a motorcycle accident and could not continue his education. For us to achieve as we did, it had to have been like threading the eye of a needle while riding a bicycle: the needle that sewed the stitch of achievement. I don't know of any other bunch of kids who were tasinques from the barrio who could claim such accomplishments. Aurelio De Leon Jr.; Richard and Norman De Leon; Frankie Hidalgo; Randy, Ruben, and Bobby Vinton; and I were those kids who were shearers.

On August 9, 2019, I went to the Rex Johnson Ranch northeast of Rocksprings. Rex was eighty-five years old at the time and had been raising Angora goats since he was sixteen. My godson, Catarino Valenzuela Jr., invited me to go with him and his shearing crew as they were to shear Johnson's eight hundred nannies and kid goats. It was a crew of eight shearers, one lanero, one empacador, and the captain, my godson. The shearers were all Hispanic, and all were older men, except one. Catarino's grandfather, Tano Aguero, ran a shearing crew for about forty-five years. Catarino took over his work and had now run the crew for over thirty years as he has carried on the Aguero tradition of working in la trasquila. However, he too sees retirement coming soon.

That day I later texted my high school classmates Cindy Winn Van Horn, Linda Vernor Ferris, Jimmie Lou Alsop Talley, and R. J. R. some pictures of the shearers. I also included pictures of the hairy Angora goats, the sheared goats, and of me shearing a goat. Their responses to my pictures were not what I expected, but I understood what they meant. Jimmie said, "The Angora will always be a favorite of mine. The kids are the cutest and the sweetest. I had a little herd of orphans I had accumulated. . . . They later helped pay for my college tuition."

Linda spoke of her pride in raising Angora goats:

My Papa, my great grandfather, was one of the past presidents of the Texas Goat Raisers Association. He was Marmaduke Taylor, known as Duke. He had a ranch in Vance, Texas. He was an unforgettable character. I have three of the silver trophies he and my grandmother won with their Angora goats. She braided the mohair before each show so the mohair would be especially beautiful. I just feel good when I see Angoras or get to talk about those days. Thanks for keeping it alive.

Cindy said, "Very poignant . . . such wonderful memories. Wish you had sent us the smells and sounds, too." She added:

The movie *The Thorn Bird* showed scenes of Australian shearing.... Those scenes were romantic and gripping—and I loved the wholesomeness, the obvious integrity and pride of the shearers. And Texas shearing was the best. Right? I am so happy you are taking on this project. It is a big part of our past (as ranchers) . . . and it is so sad to see it disappearing.

Another classmate, R. J. R., reminisced:

Shearing time was always exciting because it meant people were coming to visit. We lived so far off the beaten path, we would run to greet airplanes, thinking someone was coming to see us. Additionally, we often got to pick wool or mohair for the shearers and give them a mountain laurel bean for count that an animal had been sheared. That included your father, Leandro Aguero, and crew. Getting to "tromp" the fiber, be it wool or mohair, was always so much fun! Ultimately, rolling and jumping on the full sacks was another thrill. Because sheep and goats raised me, I feel it important to be a member of the Texas Sheep and Goat Raisers Association. Additionally, my great-grandfather John Rosenow was a charter member of the Texas Sheep and Goat Raisers Association that was formed in Del Rio at the Princess Theater. My parents, Tom and Freida Rosenow Rogers, were the reason we five Rogers kids got to happily grow up on a rough, slick, rock- and cedar-infested sheep and goat ranch in northwest Uvalde County.

Right up the road from where the Rogerses lived and down the road from where Cindy grew up, William Landrum was the first rancher who brought Angora goats to the Nueces River Valley at Laguna. I do not think Landrum was aware in 1872 that he was starting a community of Angora goat ranchers that all four of my classmates belonged to and seemingly always will, as they hold the vivid memories in their senses, and most important, in their hearts.

I understood the comments from my friends and classmates because I too had very poignant feelings during my visit to the Johnson Ranch. It was poignant in the sense that I could see and sense my community of shearers slowly disappearing. As most of the shearers were old that day, we spoke of the past, good years. We spoke of shearing on crews that sheared seventy or eighty thousand goats per season. However, they could not name one young person who was now doing the work. Instead, they spoke of their kids and grandkids being oil field workers, managers, teachers, nurses, sales people—in essence, many were professionals, but none were shearers. That day I saw the travel from ranch to ranch, the crews, the food, the camaraderie, the language, the joy of doing the work, and literally the lives of the men who did the work, all slowly disappearing.

The shearing industry still exists in Texas and the United States, but the millions of sheep and Angora goats that were once common have in large part been relegated to history. It is my hope that this book documents memories and knowledge of an industry that perhaps is not as glorified as cattle ranching but that provided nutrition, cover, and clothing for much of our nation. It also provided important work for a whole community through the industry of la trasquila.

Thus, it became almost a mission for me to capture as much of la trasquila as possible. We must leave a record of this great work and the life surrounding it. Sadly, after doing the shearing work for about ninety years, my Aguero family tradition ended in the late 1990s. My grandfather Manuel Sr. learned the skill in 1910 when he came to the United State from Sabinas, Coahuila, Mexico. He learned how to shear with hand shears. In the 1930s and 1940s he taught his sons, Leandro, Macario, Tano, Bobby, Hilario, and Manuel, the work; they progressed to shearing with machines. Our fathers, who are those men, taught my brothers Manuel and Leandro Jr. how to shear. My father passed away at the very young age of forty-seven, so he was not able to teach me; however, my brother Manuel taught me in the 1960s. In the late 1970s and the 1980s, Leandro Jr. taught his boys, Leandro III, Richard, and Eliseo.

Also in those years Manuel taught his boys Arturo and Jimmy. Being a victim of polio, his other son, Manuel "Moe" Jr., could not shear, but he was taught how to be a lanero. By then we were all shearing with electric motors powered by electric generators. The Aguero shearing generations ended with the youngest great-grandson of Manuel Aguero Sr., Eliseo Aguero. Eliseo went on to become a football coach and athletic director, but no other Aguero learned to shear after him.

I take pride in being included in the long line of Aguero shearers. I take such great pride in what I did as a goat shearer who was able to shear more than two hundred goats in one day that I will ask my son to say in my eulogy that I was just as proud of being an admired tasinque as I was of being a college president.

The long, ninety-year corte for the Agueros lasted from about 1910 to about 1995. It ended because the numbers of sheep and goats declined precipitously. Along with the decline in animals to be sheared, we and thousands of potential shearers found other work. La trasquila declined to almost extinction. Just as the time of the vaquero has run its course, the time of the full-time tasinque in Texas is gone. Let us hope that history will not forget us.

I will close by sharing a story of my pride in being a tasinque. In 1985, at the age of thirty-four, I was working as dean of instruction at Southwest Texas Junior College in Uvalde. I had traveled to Camp Wood to visit family on that Sunday. As I was driving back to Uvalde, I noticed a small crew shearing goats by the side of the road close to Laguna. It happened that one of the men shearing that day was from Uvalde, and he knew me well. As I watched the shearing, the man kiddingly said to me, "This is real work, not like office work you do." I waited for the atajo they were working on to be done. A seasoned shearer will know that once a pen full is done, the men will change cutters on the headpiece and the tools will be ready for the next bunch. The seasoned shearer also knows that the new pen full will have the best and easiest goats to shear at the beginning of the atajo. So if you choose carefully you can select a goat that can be sheared easily, since the goat will have better, finer hair that is much easier to cut off. You can usually find a goat that will have less or no mohair on its neck and little mohair on its belly, or a quatralva. These can be sheared very quickly.

I told the man, "Well, let me try to shear one to see how hard it is." I selected a quatralva, a small nanny kid goat that had fine hair. I sheared it quickly and smoothly and gave the leather strap back to the man, saying, "It doesn't seem too hard to me." The man stared in disbelief. However, the capitán said in Spanish to the man, "Don't believe this guy. He is an Aguero from Camp Wood; they are born shearers."

After so many years of not shearing, I could still do it, and I still felt great pride in doing the work, and even more in being recognized as one of a long line of Aguero men who did the work. My grandfather Manuel; my father, Leandro; my brothers, Manuel B. and Leandro Jr.; my nephews Art, Jimmy, Leandro III, Richard, and Eliseo; and I are all part of that legacy. I still feel great pride in being part of their legacy and of being a tasinque.

Glossary

As you read through the book, you will find that I use many Spanish-language words, terms, and sayings, but I also use a number of colloquial terms because that is how I learned them, experienced them, and lived them in the shearing pens of Texas and northern states such as South Dakota and Montana. For example, the words *trasquila* and *tasinque*, used throughout the book, are colloquial words as used in the shearing industry. The terms are not found in Spanish dictionaries. It is believed they were developed from either truncations of other words or from a pronunciation of how other more correct words sounded. The correct words are *trasquiladura* or *trasquilar* for *trasquila* and *trasquilador* for *tasinque*.

a lo largo. The phase of shearing as shearers take long strokes on the back of the animal.

a nombrar. To ask a girl to dance.

abuja. Literally means "needle" but used as a colloquial exclamation to the captain by shearers as they needed to stitch up an animal that had been severely cut. Correct word is *aguja*.

ahijao. Colloquial form of *ahijado,* "godson."

al reves. A method of shearing Angora goats "backward" to leave more hair on them for protection against the weather.

alcanso. Amount owed the shearer after all debts from advanced pay and other expenses had been deducted.

amarador. Person who tied the wool fleeces before they were packed into the large sacks.

amolador. Person who sharpened the tools for the shearers.

aprendiz. Beginner or apprentice shearer.

arrastrado. Literally means "to slither," but the term was used for lazy persons.

arreglaban. The process by which the captain and shearer reconcile the shearer's earnings, expenses, and pay.

atajo. A pen full of animals brought into the shearing pen to be sheared.

atole. A porridge made of oatmeal or rice.

atole de arroz. Rice porridge.

baile. A dance celebration.

baratero. Term applied to a captain who may undercut another captain by offering a lower price for shearing a rancher's animals.

barrio. Neighborhood generally found in largely Hispanic communities.

bien miedosa. A woman who is prone to be scared of things.

Bola, lanero. Expression shearers used to call the person who picked up the fleece or mohair.

boléro. A slow Spanish dance.

buey. Ox, used in derision of another person but generally in jest.

caballo. Horse.

cachucha. Colloquial word meaning "a cap" but was used by shearers when they sheared one more animal than their competitor.

Caló. A jargon spoken by *pachucos* and others in the United States.

capasete. Cape of mohair that went unsheared on an Angora goat's back for protection from the weather.

capitán. The shearing crew captain.

carne. Literally means "meat" but was used as an expression for the meat the rancher provided to the shearers.

cenizo. Purple sagebrush.

chale con ese jale. Expression used by *pachucos* to mean "nix with that job."

Chicano. A person of Mexican descent but used to describe Hispanic music in this book.

chino. The shearing comb.

cocinero. The cook for the shearing crew.

coleando. Colloquial term for the phase of shearing in which the tail area of the Angora goat is being sheared.

compadres. Co-fathers.

companía. The shearing crew, as in *la companía de Tano Aguero.*

con corazón. With heart and emotion.

corralero. The person who drove/pushed/herded the animals into the shearing pen.

cuantas. How many? The captain asked this question of shearers to see how many they had sheared that day.

Cuantas estaran dicendo, "Si ese hombre fuera sido mi marido?" How many women must be saying, "If only that man had been my husband?"

cuidar las esquinas. Watch or take care of the corners of the shearing pen.

cumbia. Salsa-type music.

cuñao. Colloquial form of *cuñado*, which means "brother-in-law."

de campo. To camp out while shearing at a ranch.

Despues le mando una notita. I'll send you a little note later.

desgraciado. Literally means "disgraced" but was used by shearers in jest or to signify someone who was very good at something.

desorillo. Tagging sheep, which meant to shear only their face, udder, and anal area.

dispuntar. To remove or blunt the overly sharp points on a shearing comb.

distintivos. The pieces of ribbons or tickets pinned on a man's collar to indicate that he had paid as he entered a dance hall.

docientero. A shearer who could shear more than two hundred animals in one day.

El apetito es el mejor cocinero. A good appetite is the best cook.

El Cañon. Literally means "the canyon"; the name given by the Spaniards in the 1700s to the Nueces River Canyon.

El cocinero debe de matar los chivos, tu no. The cook should slaughter the goats, not you.

el corte chiquito. The short shearing season, generally from early July to the end of September.

el corte largo. The long shearing season, generally from February to the end of June.

el norte. The north country.

El que mucho habla poco logra. He who talks much accomplishes little.

el rancho de los blanquillos. The ranch of the eggs (colloquial).

el rancho del gorrudo. The ranch of the man with the big hat.

el rancho del paralis. The ranch of the man who was paralyzed.

El trabajo es la mejor cama. Work makes the best bed.

empacador. The person who packs the wool or mohair into the large sacks.

empacadora. The packing machine contraption.

En cada cabeza un mundo. In each head another world.

enganche. Money advanced to shearers before the shearing season starts.

enganchista. Person who seeks to contract shearers by advancing them money before the shearing season starts.

Estas muy feo. You are too ugly.

extra. The shearer who moved from one station to another when there were not enough stations for all the shearers.

frijolillo. Mountain laurel bean, sometimes used as a token for shearing.

golpe. An exclamation used to warn shearers that animals were loose and might run into them.

grito. A yell or exclamation made with great exultation.

guapango. A dance such as the Mexican hat dance.

hacienda. A Mexican ranch or settlement.

ingenio. Name for the shearing machine in the era in which it was located on a truck.

jugando pesado. Literally means "playing very heavily"; indicated bantering with other shearers in a very strong fashion but always in jest.

jugavan bien pesado. Engaged in "heavy joking."

Juntan lana. Do you pick up wool?

la espada. Title given to the shearer on the crew who sheared the most animals in one day.

La Llorona. The wailing woman who roams the rivers looking for her lost children; generally referred to as a legend in Hispanic culture.

la loba. The last animal to be sheared in a pen full.

la mera sorga. The "best of best" shearers.

La Villa. Name given by Hispanics in Camp Wood to the town of Barksdale.

lambusco. Used by shearers to signify a person who was a "brown-noser."

Lambusco, vete de una vez. Brown-noser, go ahead and leave now.

lanero. The person who picked up the wool or mohair and took it to the packing machine.

Las Hermanitas Ranch. Name of a ranch in South Texas, meaning "the little sisters ranch."

latifundio. A ranching empire consisting of various ranches under one ownership.

Le corrio al cápitan. He ran from the captain.

Le pido a Dios que me deje llegar a cien años. I ask God to let me live to be one hundred years old.

Llano Estacado. Palisaded plains of Texas.

lobero. A shearer who was deft at avoiding *la loba*, the last animal to be sheared in a pen full.

lonche frio. A cold lunch.

los alemanes. Literally means "the Germans"; name of a pasture on the Silver Lake Ranch.

manadas. Herds of animals.

mande. Literally means "order me"; a form of responding with great respect for the person calling one's name (for instance, if one's mother called, one did not respond with *¿que?* [what?] but *mande*).

mango. The shearing headpiece.

máquina. Literally means a "machine" but used to signify to whom the crew belonged, such as *la máquina de Frank Hidalgo.*

Me debes una. You owe me one.

Me puede hacer mal. It could make me sick.

merienda. The coffee and snack break taken by shearers, generally about 4.00 p.m.

Mexicano. A man from Mexico.

moyejón. The metal spinning disc used to sharpen the shearer's tools.

muy buena gente. Very good people.

navaja. The shearing cutters.

Nel no lo metemos toda en el pedo. We spend it all on partying.

No heran reglistas. They were not complainers.

No lloro porque te vas, lloro porque not te as ido. I'm not crying because you are leaving; I'm crying because you have not left yet.

No te preocupes, nomas son moscas. Don't worry, they are only flies.

Norias Dobles. Literally means "double wells"; name of a sub-ranch on the Silver Lake Ranch.

Nuestra Señora de la Candelaria. Name of the mission the Spaniards established in the 1700s at Montell, Texas.

ocho manos. Eight hands; used to signify how many stations/drops there were on the shearing machine.

pachucos. A group of individuals generally of Hispanic origin who dressed distinctly and spoke a special language of their own; the language was sometimes *Caló*.

pan de campo. Camp bread.

pansiando. Shearing the belly of the animal.

Pero mañana vamos andar en el baile, tomando cerveza pero bien helada. But tomorrow we will be at the dance, drinking really really cold beer.

pescuesiando. Shearing the neck of the animal.

pistolas. Pistols.

polka. A form of dance with German and/or Polish origins.

Por dinero baila el chango. The monkey dances for money.

por la desgraciada tomada. Because of that damn drinking.

pora. A colloquial term used to designate the man who assisted the captain.

puyistas. Shearers who used double entendre or innuendo to belittle others in jest.

quarteando. Shearing up to a quarter of an animal.

quatralvas. Animals who had little mohair or wool on their stomach and neck; favored by shearers since they could be sheared quickly.

Que alma de hombre para trasquilar. What a soul that man had for shearing.

quinceañera. A celebration held when a young woman reaches the age of fifteen.

ranchero. Rancher.

rata. Literally means "rat"; the title given to the shearer on the crew who sheared the least animals in a day.

reganchados. Colloquial term for shearers who were now under contract since they received advanced pay.

reganche. Colloquial term for pay advanced to the shearer before the shearing season began.

reglistas. A pejorative term used for shearers who had many demands or complaints while on the shearing crews.

remedios. Home remedies.

repepena. Colloquial term used to signify the animals that were left unsheared after the crew had left; shearers had to return later to shear those animals.

Río de las Nueces. Name given by the Spaniards to the Nueces River of Texas, literally, "River of the Pecans."

rosarios. Rosaries.

sacando dinero. Taking out money; used to signify a situation whereby a shearer asked the captain for money during the shearing season.

Salud, dinero, y amor y tiempo para gozarlos. Health, money, and love and time to enjoy them.

San Lorenzo de la Santa Cruz. Name of the Spanish mission the Spaniards established in the 1700s at Camp Wood.

sancho. The lead animal used to guide the others into the shearing pen.

Se agaraban bien a bien. They would get after it.

sentando. Phase of shearing when the animal is "sat" by the shearer.

Si asi fueran pa trabajar. If only you could work that good.

sin pelos en la lengua. Literally means "without hairs on the tongue"; used to indicate, "I will not mince my words."

soltar patras. Colloquial term used by shearers when they released a sheared animal behind them rather than to their front.

suegro. Father-in-law.

tasinque. A shearer.

tecole. A tarry mixture of alcohol and other healing substances applied to the cuts of the animals that could occur as they were being sheared.

tecolero. The person who applied the *tecole*.

Tejanos. Hispanic people born in Texas; also a genre of music.

Tejas. Spanish name for the state of Texas.

tesonero. The title given to the shearer who was not the fastest but who sheared very well every day of the season.

tijeras trincas. The scissor-type shears used in the early days.

trasquila. The shearing industry.

trasquilar. To shear.

vaquero. A cowboy of Hispanic origin.

Vente angelon de la guardia. Come on, big guardian angel.

voces. voices.

welo. A colloquial term truncated from the word *abuelo*, which means "grandfather." The diminutive form is *welito*.

References

Albin, Rick L. 2002. *The Sheep Shearing Contractors of Uvalde County and Their Tokens*. Uvalde: Self-published.

Alonzo, Armando C. 1998. *Tejano Legacy: Rancheros and Settlers in South Texas 1734–1900*. Albuquerque: University of New Mexico Press.

Anonymous. 1885. "Sheep-Shearing on a Texas Ranch." *San Angelo Standard Times*.

Arreola, Daniel D. 2002. *Tejano South Texas: A Mexican American Cultural Province*. Austin: University of Texas Press.

Ballesteros, Octavio A., and Maria del Carmen Ballesteros. 1992. *Mexican Sayings: The Treasure of a People*. Austin: Eakin Press.

Brezosky, Lynn. 2018a. "Greater Demand for a Little Lamb." *San Antonio Express and News*, February 11.

———. 2018b. "Hill Country Sheep and Goat Ranchers Find a Hot Market." *San Antonio Express and News*, May 5.

Carlson, Paul H. 1982. *Texas Woollybacks: The Range Sheep and Goat Industry*. College Station: Texas A&M University Press.

———. 2010. *Sheep Ranching*. Austin: Texas State Historical Association.

Crisp, Margie. 2017. *The Nueces River: Rio Escondido*. College Station: Texas A&M University Press.

De León, Arnoldo. 1982. *The Tejano Community, 1836–1900*. Albuquerque: University of New Mexico Press.

———. 1985. *San Angeleños: Mexican Americans in San Angelo, Texas*. San Angelo: Fort Concho Museum Press.

———. 2015. *Tejano West Texas*. College Station: Texas A&M University Press.

Del Castillo, Richard Griswold, and Arnoldo De León. 1997. *North to Aztlan: A History of Mexican Americans in the United States*. New York: Twayne Publishers.

Dominguez, Bertha. 2004. "Welito: A Mexican-American Family in Southwest Texas." In *Both Sides of the Border: A Scattering of Texas Folklore*, edited by Edward Francis and Kenneth L Untiedt, 57–64. Denton: University of North Texas Press.

Duran, Livie Isauro, and Russell H. Bernard. 1973. *Introduction to Chicano Studies*. New York: Macmillan.

Fehrenbach, T. R. 1983. *Seven Keys to Texas*. El Paso: University of Texas at El Paso Press.

Fenly, Florence. 1967. "Old Trails." *Uvalde Leader News*.

Fisher, O. C. 1985. *The Speaker of Nubbin Ridge*. San Angelo: Talley Press.

Garcia, Lionel. 2004. *Brush Country*. Huntsville: Texas Review Press.

Gladwell, Malcolm. 2008. *Outliers: The Story of Success*. New York: Little, Brown.

Guerrero, Salvador. 1991. *Memorias: A West Texas Life*. Lubbock: Texas Tech University Press.

Harris, Charles H., III. 1975. *A Mexican Family Empire: The Latifundios of the Sanchez Navarros, 1765–1867*. Austin: University of Texas Press.

Hart, Elva Trevino. 1999. *Barefoot Heart: Stories of a Migrant Child*. Tempe, AZ: Bilingual Press: Editorial Bilingue.

Hayes, John, L. 1868. *The Angora Goat: Its Origin, Culture and Products*. Boston: Press of A. A. Kingman.

Hill, Billy Bob. 1994. *Texas in Poetry*. Denton: University of North Texas.

Jones, Lem. 1995. *Angora Goats, Then and Now: 1849 to 1995*. Austin: Nortex Press.

Kelton, Elmer. 2007. "Ranching in a Changing Land." In *Texas Almanac*, edited by Elizabeth Cruce Alvarez. Austin: Texas State Historical Association.

Kupper, Winifred. 1945. *The Golden Hoof: The Story of the Sheep of the Southwest*. New York: Alfred A Knopf.

Lehmann, V. W. 1969. *Forgotten Legions: Sheep in the Rio Grande Plain of Texas*. El Paso: Texas Western Press, University of Texas at El Paso.

Martinez, Monica Muñoz. 2018. *The Injustice Never Leaves You: Anti-Mexican Violence in Texas*. Cambridge, MA: Harvard University Press.

Maudslay, Robert. 1951. *Texas Sheepman: The Reminiscences of Robert Maudslay*. Austin: University of Texas Press.

McSwain, Ross. 1996. *Texas Sheep & Goat Raisers Association 1915–1995: A History of Service*. San Angelo: Anchor Publishing.

McWilliams, Carey. 1990. *North from Mexico: The Spanish-Speaking People of the United States*. Updated by Matt S. Meier. New York: Praeger Publishers.

Mohair Council of America. n.d. *Mohair Production and Marketing*. San Angelo: Mohair Council of America.

Murphy, Colin. 2019. "A Legacy Cut Short: San Angelo Sheep Shearers Are the Last of Their Kind." *San Angelo Standard Times*, October 14.

Opdyke, Jeff D. 1998. "Mohair Ranchers Feel the Pain of Lost Federal Subsidies." *Wall Street Journal*, April 1.

Perkins, Barbara. 2018. *Shattered Spring: The People's Story of the F5 Tornado That Ravaged Rocksprings, Texas*. Rocksprings: Barbara Perkins Publisher.

Reinhold, Robert. 1985. "Texas Ranchers 'Shear' Gold from Angora Goats." *New York Times*, November 16.

Roberts, Ken. 2018. *The Cedar Choppers: Life on the Edge of Nothing.* College Station: Texas A&M University Press.

Saenz, Andres. 1999. *Early Tejano Ranching: Daily Life at Ranchos San Jose & El Fresnillo.* College Station: Texas A&M University Press.

Salmon, D. E. 1892. *Special Report on the History and Present Condition of the Sheep Industry of the United States, 1892.* Washington, DC: Government Printing Office.

Sanchez, George I. 1949. *Study of the Spanish-Speaking People of Texas.* Austin: University of Texas Press.

Sanchez, Saul. 2014. *Rows of Memory: Journeys of a Migrant Sugar-Beet Worker.* Iowa City: University of Iowa Press.

Shelton, Maurice. 1993. *Angora Goat and Mohair Production.* San Angelo: Anchor Publishing.

Stovall, Allan A. 1952. *Nueces Headwater Country: A Regional History.* San Antonio: Naylor.

———. 1967. *Pioneer Days in the Breaks of the Balcones: A Regional History.* Austin: Firm Foundation Publishing House.

Thompson, George Fayette. 1901. *Information concerning the Angora Goat.* Washington, DC: Government Printing Office.

Tijerina, Andres. 1998. *Tejano Empire: Life on the South Texas Ranchos.* College Station: Texas A&M University Press.

Wentworth, Edward Norris. 1948. *America's Sheep Trails: History, Personalities.* Ames: Iowa State College Press.

Whittley, Sandy. 2002. *List of Shearing Captains.* San Angelo: Texas Sheep & Goat Raisers Association Publishers.

Wilkes, Stephany. 2018. *Raw Material: Working Wool in the West.* Corvallis: Oregon State University Press.

Unpublished Interviews by Robert Aguero

Aguero, Manuel, Jr. 2019. Camp Wood, Texas, August 28.

Davis, John Allen (Jad), Jr. 2020. Davis Ranch, Rio Frio, Texas, October 26.

Earwood, Edward. 2020. Earwood Ranch, Sonora, Texas, October 8.

Hidalgo, Gandy. 2019. Camp Wood, Texas, August 1.

Martinez, Felipe Valverde. 2019. Brackettville, Texas, September 13.

Ross, Joe David. 2020. Sonora, Texas, October 3.

Index